THE PATHOLOGY OF
THE ENGLISH RENAISSANCE

STUDIES IN THE HISTORY
OF
CHRISTIAN THOUGHT

EDITED BY

HEIKO A. OBERMAN, Tucson, Arizona

IN COOPERATION WITH

HENRY CHADWICK, Cambridge
JAROSLAV PELIKAN, New Haven, Connecticut
BRIAN TIERNEY, Ithaca, New York
ARJO VANDERJAGT, Groningen

VOLUME LXXXVI

ELIZABETH MAZZOLA

THE PATHOLOGY OF
THE ENGLISH RENAISSANCE

THE PATHOLOGY OF
THE ENGLISH RENAISSANCE

SACRED REMAINS AND HOLY GHOSTS

BY

ELIZABETH MAZZOLA

BRILL
LEIDEN · BOSTON · KÖLN
1998

This book is printed on acid-free paper.

Library of Congress Cataloging-in-Publication Data

Mazzola, Elizabeth.
  The pathology of the English Renaissance : sacred remains and holy
ghosts / by Elizabeth Mazzola.
    p. cm. — (Studies in the history of Christian thought, ISSN
0081-8607 ; v. 86)
  Includes bibliographical references and indexes.
  ISBN 9004111956 (hardcover : alk. paper)
  1. English literature—Early modern, 1500-1700—History and
criticism. 2. Christianity and literature—England—History—16th
century. 3. Christianity and literature—England—History—17th
century. 4. Christian literature—English—History and criticism.
5. Medievalism—England—History—16th century. 6. Medievalism-
-England—History—17th century. 7. Protestantism and literature.
8. Holy, The, in literature. 9. Renaissance—England.
10. Reformation—England   I. Title.   II. Series.
PR428.C48M39   1998
820.9'3823'09031—dc21   98-25295
                                                                CIP

Die Deutsche Bibliothek - CIP-Einheitsaufnahme

Mazzola, Elizabeth:
The pathology of the English Renaissance : sacred remains and holy
ghosts / by Elizabeth Mazzola. – Leiden ; Boston ; Köln : Brill, 1998
  (Studies in the history of Christian thought ; Vol. 86)
  ISBN 90–04–11195–6

ISSN 0081-8607
ISBN 90 04 11195 6

PRINTED IN THE NETHERLANDS

TABLE OF CONTENTS

ACKNOWLEDGMENTS

I have been graced to know the friendship of many students and scholars. This book is richer because of their suggestions, on shakier ground when I have stubbornly persisted in going my own way. My husband James Picerno has sweetly nourished my soul; in the long year that I have been obsessed with tracking remains, he has consistently held out the promise of beginning again. The sustained support provided by The Wegman Fund and City College Dean Martin Tamny helped me to care for this project through all of its stages. A CCNY Rifkind Fellowship and two Professional Staff Congress-CUNY research awards made possible much of the time I took to think and rewrite. Raphael Falco has been a Doric column of support, a never-fading emblem of friendship. I am grateful to The Spenser Society which awarded me its 1996 Isabel MacCaffrey prize, and to The Folger Shakespeare Library for a generous summer stipend in 1995. Kate D. Levin listened to several incarnations of arguments about transubstantiation and supplied me with the idea of "untransubstantiated hosts," as well as numberless ideas and questions and immeasurable aid. She has kept the winds of enthusiasm blowing in my direction. My brother Steven Mazzola could always be counted on to share ideas, and he carefully responded to a range of questions about dramaturgy, performance theory, and staging.

Professor Heiko A. Oberman, editor of this series "Studies in the History of Christian Thought," has been an unremitting source of encouragement, provocation and kindness. I also am indebted to Marit Alberts, Gera van Bedaf, and Dr. M.G. Elisabeth Venekamp at Brill Academic Publishers for their ready answers and care. Norman Kelvin and Laura Hinton took upon themselves the heavy labor of reading drafts of chapters. Fred Reynolds, Paul Sherwin and Paul Oppenheimer shared many insights, reminding me of what to emphasize, what to leave out, how to think about nuts and bolts, audiences and readers. When the argument was in its preliminary stages, I received much useful advice from readers like Ralph V. Norman, R.A. Shoaf, Susan Green, and Jon Quitslund. Early teachers Arthur Kirsch, Ernest B. Gilman and Harold Bloom helped me in and out of wandering woods. I also drew on the assistance of learned colleagues like Douglas Brooks, N.I. Matar, Philip

Beitchman, Debora Shuger and Barbara Fisher. David G. Mark probed some of the deeper questions. Susanne Wofford, Kenneth Gross, Maureen Quilligan, Elizabeth Bellamy and Gordon Teskey were especially generous with their counsel and interest; they served both as implied and actual readers along the way.

The community of Spenserians at Kalamazoo, particularly David Miller and Jon Quitslund, has provided a crucial forum for exchange and good will. Equally important were chances to share ideas at forums sponsored by The Modern Language Association, The New York University Seminar on the Renaissance, The City College Renaissance Discussion Group, The Society for the Study of Women in the Renaissance, and The International Congress on Medieval Studies. I must also thank Johan R.M. Jensen and Poul Grinder-Hansen of the National Museum of Denmark, the interlibrary loan department at The Cohen Library of City College, the English Department of New York University, and Theresa Helein and the staff at The Folger Shakespeare Library.

Some parts of this book were first published elsewhere, and I am obliged to the editors and publishers who have graciously allowed me to reprint materials here. I thank Ralph V. Norman and the University of Tennessee for allowing me to reprint sections from Chapter 1, which first appeared as "Apocryphal Texts and Epic Amnesia" in *Soundings* 78,1 (Spring 1995); Susan Green, who allowed me to reprint a version of Chapter 2 which appeared as "Ethical Dilemmas and Romance Destinations in *The Faerie Queene*" in *The Huntington Library Quarterly* 60,3 (1997); Charles Durham, Kris McColgan, and Susquehanna University Press, for allowing me to reprint part of chapter 3 which will appear as "Milton's Eve as Closed Corpus and Apocryphal Text" in *"All in All": Unity, Diversity, and the Miltonic Perspective*.

My students at City College have been the first and last audience for my ideas and experiments, the inspiration and prime movers behind them; they have supplied me with countless lessons in "vertuous and gentle discipline," and I am always grateful for their expert guidance. But my parents were my first teachers, and to them this book is lovingly dedicated.

E.M.
The City College of New York
March 1998

ILLUSTRATIONS

INTRODUCTION

In the course of more important projects, cultures routinely discard symbols and other imaginative habits. But abandoned symbols or practices do not simply disappear from the mental landscape; and sometimes, this discarded material takes up far more space. No longer scrutinized so carefully or clung to as dearly as official public knowledge, outworn symbols can find their powers increased by occupying the margins of accepted ideas, shadowing the background of the imagination. The anthropologist Mary Douglas suggests that cultural "flotsam and jetsam" are often forced into "pigeonholes of oblivion," black holes of memory which house an arsenal of "natural symbols" or "implicit meanings." It is the deeper structure those implicit meanings create which allows more explicit meanings and obvious symbols to be read.[1] But this means we are educated about what to forget, as well.

Douglas's argument suggests an afterlife for abandoned symbols that Michel Foucault's archaeology of knowledge seems to ignore. According to his account in *The Order of Things*, *epistemes* or regimes of knowledge outlaw certain forms of reasoning in the process of making possible other forms.[2] Hans Blumenberg portrays those intellectual procedures, ones we tend to regard in terms of progress, as systematic and irrational. Blumenberg also claims that modern reason was forced into a detour when made to "reoccupy" outmoded philosophical solutions and, thus, provide answers to transcendental problems long since repudiated.[3] The knowledge that is banished becomes simply "impossible" or "unthinkable"; converted into myth or superstition, this suppressed data reappears as a set of ideas not only anachronistic but false.[4] Still, its diminished status does not prevent "impossible" knowledge from affecting behaviors

---

[1] See Mary Douglas, *Natural Symbols: Explorations in Cosmology* and *Implicit Meanings: Essays in Anthropology*.

[2] Michel Foucault, *The Order of Things: An Archaeology of the Human Sciences*.

[3] Hans Blumenberg, *The Legitimacy of the Modern Age*.

[4] Timothy Reiss describes these "impossible knowledges" in *The Discourse of Modernism*. See also Blumenberg, *Work on Myth*. Andrew Delbanco similarly chronicles the modern evolution of transcendental mechanisms in *The Death of Satan: How Americans Have Lost the Sense of Evil*.

or perceptions altogether. Citing Jung, Alastair Fowler likewise notes that "past experience . . . is far from passive or inert. Cultural 'remains' are seldom mere detritus, at least psychologically: more often they are very active."[5] Perhaps these remains have such powerful effects on the moral imagination because they make so few claims on it.

Nevertheless, the disowning of cognitive stances or epistemological frameworks can cause tremendous psychic pain, as when twentieth-century behavioralists discount readings of the past offered by psychoanalysts. Debates about forms of knowledge and the traumas these debates provoke have run still deeper, abolishing an even wider array of memories. As I suggest in this book, in the habits and projects of the Renaissance are some of the most self-consciously sophisticated methodologies for the burial and retrieval of cultural knowledge. The "classics" are recovered and a Bible assembled from newly-translated Greek texts; at the same time, however, religion is isolated as a cultural artifact, a body of knowledge to be debated, clarified or, with reason, set aside. Such developments would seem to emerge out of the secular impulses of the period, although I will argue otherwise; at the moment, it might suffice to note that the term "secular" describes time as something divided into "ages" or "eras," and so usefully indicates how religion could now recognize—and wrestle with—its history. In the chapters that follow, I examine some of the beginnings of this anguished history. Tracing the fate of lost symbols or discarded beliefs after the Protestant reformation, I explore what might be called the pathology of the Renaissance.

∗∗∗

Literary critics and church historians like Debora K. Shuger, Jerome Friedman, Eamon Duffy, and Timothy Reiss have also commented on the complex practices of cultural burial and retrieval

---

[5] Alastair Fowler, *Time's Purpled Masquers: Stars and the Afterlife in Renaissance English Literature* (3-4). Cf. Julia Reinhard Lupton, *Afterlives of the Saints: Hagiography, Typology, and Renaissance Literature*. Lupton proposes that secularism 'annuls' Christianity" (xviii). I would argue, in contrast, that secularism's effects are more benign, at times even productive, because secularism rewrites Christianity. As a set of symbols, Christianity can either be widened or emptied out, never voided completely.

I explore here, and suggested that the Renaissance imagination was sharply defined by ideas reformers forced it to repudiate.[6] But my book pushes this possibility even further, arguing that Renaissance literature teaches Protestant theology to recognize what it can do, and what it can do without. I propose that sacred symbols and practices still powerfully organized the English moral imagination in the sixteenth and seventeenth centuries, continued to orient behaviors and arrange perceptions, and persisted in specifying to believers and non-believers alike the limits of the known world. These sacred symbols remained the primary guides to and deepest structures for feeling; and the machinery which replaces them almost a century later (including experimental methods, calculus and statistics, and anatomical demonstrations) will instead provide a wider range of techniques for registering reality more fully.

Analyzing the potent traces of religious motives and symbols in the sixteenth and seventeenth centuries, John Guillory maintains that the Renaissance literary imagination takes up precisely where sacred inspiration leaves off.[7] Whether the Reformation air simply gets thinner or, as Spenser proposes, the saint's view of New Jerusalem gradually recedes, literary goals become increasingly authoritative and scriptural at this time. As Shuger claims, only the shape, not the nature of orthodoxy keeps changing.[8]

One might consider the evolution of the English literary tradition as the carefully-protracted unearthing of a site where authority can find itself. The works of Spenser, Shakespeare, and Milton in particular manage to recollect discarded symbols and sacred remains and to preserve ideas that are meaningful but irrelevant. These powerful relics come to inhabit a "separative cognitive zone."[9] Northrop Frye has similarly construed romance as a kind of "secular scripture" because it protects cultural discards or ruins by

---

[6] Debora K. Shuger, *Habits of Thought in the English Renaissance: Religion, Politics, & the Dominant Culture*; Jerome Friedman, *The Most Ancient Testimony: Sixteenth-Century Christian-Hebraica in the Age of Renaissance Nostalgia*; Eamon Duffy, *The Stripping of the Altars*; Reiss (1982).

[7] John Guillory, *Poetic Authority: Spenser, Milton, and Literary History*.

[8] See Shuger (1990). Perhaps this process duplicates the cartographical mapping of the Renaissance world. In *Geography of Religions*, David E. Sopher argues that because of religious change the dimensions of the earth are continually reorganized.

[9] I borrow the phrase from Frank Kermode, "The Canon." *The Literary Guide to the Bible* (606).

relocating them to safer climes.[10] Under a strictly-literary rubric, however, a symbol's moral value or theological weight tends to be less and less crucial to its interpretation. If More's *Utopia* is careful to enumerate its many pretensions, the Renaissance canon serves literally as good place and no place.

***

My emphasis on the continued role of disowned symbols develops the suggestions of New Historicist critics like Stephen Greenblatt who propose that subversive ideas were managed or contained during the Renaissance by dominant literary texts.[11] But there are some notable differences between my claims and Greenblatt's. Most importantly, my study concentrates on ideas that were publicly acknowledged to be false or groundless or unpersuasive, like Catholic conceptions about purgatory and transubstantiation. Simply put, these ideas–along with the symbols they employ and the practices they encourage–no longer work: they fail to describe reality, while ignoring other cultural requirements for meaning, power or guidance. Rather than actively continuing to shape texts or readers, these ideas constitute a secret record of the imagination's failures or an arrangement of its lies. In the same way that Latin becomes a dead language,[12] these dead or dying symbols become poetry, according to Philip Sidney's dictum not even pretending to truth.

The other qualification is that not all symbols were evacuated or abandoned altogether. The Reformation universe could still be navigated by Catholics with a scaled-down version of their ethos or world-view, which had become, by the sixteenth century, bloated and murky. One oft-criticized Catholic excess was the medieval system of indulgences repudiated by Luther. Under its generous provisions, sacred debts mandated by Lenten rules or otherworldly sentences were discharged by papal pardons in exchange for the payments of sinners.[13] Typically, indulgences guaranteed one's choice

---

[10] Northrop Frye, *The Secular Scripture: A Study of the Structure of Romance.*

[11] See Stephen Greenblatt, *Renaissance Self-Fashioning from More to Shakespeare.*

[12] See G. W. Pigman, III, "Imitation and the Renaissance sense of the past: the reception of Erasmus' *Ciceronianus.*" (169).

[13] The few sins papal pardons could not excuse included bigamy and voluntary murder. See Arthur J. Slavin, "The Gutenberg Galaxy and the Tudor Revolution." *Print and Culture in the Renaissance: Essays on the Advent of Printing in Europe* (90-109).

of confessor or ensured a Christian burial in time of interdict, but in some cases an indulgence could commute an otherworldly sentence. One Richard Erle, for instance, received a remission of eight thousand years. Like the monies paid to ransom relatives from Turkish captivity, by 1476 indulgences could be used to release family members from purgatory.[14] Not only was the system subject to insincerity or flat-out corruption, but sin was becoming profitable, with payment accepted in installments and advertisements for pardons promising that these privileges would never expire.

In addition, Elizabeth Eisenstein reports, the Church often repaid printers of indulgences with indulgences, so that pardons "became almost equivalent to currency";[15] when bound with dictionaries, they would also be employed as necessary lexical tools.[16] In fact, we might locate a wealth of indulgences the Church granted, ecclesiastical techniques for extending human powers beyond the grave or reducing God's powers in heaven. Such imaginative way stations or escape hatches had innumerable effects on medieval economies, cartographies, visual arts, reading habits, holidays, work practices, and domestic routines, even as the money collected erected countless roads and hospitals and churches.[17] Indulgences had effects on other worlds, too. The invention (or intervention) of purgatory eased the transition between this world and the next by collapsing the "unthinkable" difference between the living and the dead and the fierce absolutism dividing heaven from hell.[18] For this reason, more than a century after the doctrine was officially rejected, Samuel Johnson still found it necessary to expose purgatory as a false stronghold. It was not that purgatory merely upset ontolo-

[14] According to Rev. Prebendary Clark-Maxwell, Richard Erle's case was an exception to the "general tenor" of indulgences. See "Some Further Letters of Fraternity," *Archaeologia, or, Miscellaneous tracts relating to Antiquity* (204). Also see Elizabeth L. Eisenstein, *The printing press as an agent of change* (376); and Albert Way, "Notice of a Formula of a Papal Indulgence, Printed by Pynson, and of some other documents of like character" (255).

[15] Eisenstein 376 n252.

[16] Way 250-56.

[17] See Edward Ingebretsen, *Maps of Heaven, Maps of Hell.* Fowler (1996) likewise describes the implications of abandoning the Ptolemaic system: "Reordering the planets meant altering the entire intellectual world—metaphors, memory systems, encyclopedias, and all" (39-40).

[18] John Bossy, *Christianity in the West 1400-1700* (56); Jacques Le Goff, *The Birth of Purgatory.*

gies or contradicted biblical teachings, but that it professed too
many powers for metonymy, and Johnson condemned purgatory as
a "Doctrine of the Poets" who fancied that "one man's taking
Physick should make another man Well."[19]

The elevation of the eucharistic host during the Latin mass
should be viewed as another imaginative indulgence, making the
Godhead visible exactly at the moment of its sacrifice. Seventeenth-
century Catholic John Lechmere defended the doctrine of the "Real
Presence" against reformers who condemned Catholicism as a
"iugling philosophie"–promising to make Christ's absent body reappear at the mass, only to disappear once again in the mouths of
communicants.[20] Rejecting purgatory or limiting the number of
masses a priest might offer (and thus the number of times Christ's
body would reappear), Protestant reform employs a "disjunctive,
antimagical semiotics" to contract or demystify such notions and
challenge the charged sacramental language of Catholicism that
permits "the signifier to act upon the world of referents."[21]

Although the Renaissance vocabulary had not shrunken, then, its
powers were severely delimited. John Bossy explains how the confusing medieval image of the Seven Deadly sins was displaced at
this time by the clear-cut rules prescribed by the Ten
Commandments. Chaucer's Pardoner's Tale would lose its footing
in the foreshortened universe of Protestantism, but perhaps it would
also entice fewer listeners to sin.[22]

***

So scandalous to the Protestant imagination was not the splitting of
Catholic energies between this world and the next, but the conceit
that Catholic symbols could make themselves disappear altogether.
Yet Protestant stories did not empty or destroy Catholic ones: the
breaks were more carefully orchestrated, less thorough-going, and
less damaging. A more persuasive trope for these ruptures than the

---

[19] Samuel Johnson, *Purgatory prov'd by miracles collected out of Roman-Catholick Authors.*

[20] See John Lechmere, *The Relection of a Conference Touching the Reall Presence (1635) English Recusant Literature 1558-1640* (140).

[21] Thomas M. Greene, "Introduction," *Ceremony and Text in the Renaissance* (12-13).

[22] Bossy (1989) 37-38.

one offered by iconoclastic smashing is provided by the reformers' reading of the eucharist as mnemonic device. The Protestant imagination was inspired by a lingering set of sacred remains, organized by a store of symbols to be interpreted piece-by-piece, rather than consumed entirely.

For this reason, the Protestant world is coated with symbolic residue, like Hamlet's father's ghost or the corpses which litter Spenser's *Faerie Queene*, rotting signs which also include King Arthur himself. This imaginative decay leads Patrick Collinson to claim that "English Protestantism . . . produced no culture of its own but made an iconoclastic holocaust of the culture which already existed."[23] But this is an unfortunate misreading. The pervasiveness of such residue does not denude or enfeeble Protestant story-telling, for cultures cannot be depleted by their histories. This is something biblical scholar John Cosin inadvertently makes clear in his *Scholastical History* (1657) when he tells us that Catholics used the "untruly" term "Novelists" to describe Protestants' designs. To be sure, their term is inappropriate: not only suspicious but incapable of the totalizing claims of the sacred, Protestantism will multiply fragments and partial signs that only, in the reader's mind, resemble a larger whole. If Hamlet decides to stage a play himself at Elsinore, another reformist solution was to collect these stray bits and pieces, as William Camden does in his *Remains Concerning Britain* (1605), thereby circumscribing the "rude rubble and out-cast rubbish" excluded from his chorographical history *Britannia*.[24]

Hamlet's *Mousetrap* and Camden's assemblage introduce other questions, however. Given two versions of history or two collections of data, which story becomes antique or outmoded? Which image supplants—or consoles for the loss of—the other?

Spenser's *Epithalamion* (1594) endlessly circles these uncertainties. A wedding poem written to celebrate the poet's (second) marriage, it obsessively supplies cosmic assurances in place of the blessings previously guaranteed by a sacramental view of marriage.[25] Absent

---

[23] Patrick Collinson, *The Birthpangs of Protestant England: Religious and Cultural Change in the Sixteenth and Seventeenth Centuries* (94).

[24] William Camden, *Remains Concerning Britain*. The "rude" "rubbish" Camden collects primarily includes linguistic artifacts: surnames, "impreses," "wise speeches," and proverbs.

[25] See Elizabeth Mazzola, "Marrying Medusa: Spenser's *Epithalamion* and Renaissance Reconstructions of Female Privacy."

in Spenser's poem is any mention of the wedding ring formerly
blessed by the priest during the nuptial mass, the most obvious symbol of ceremonial circularity, as well as of the new and unbreakable
alliance of the lovers.[26] In its place, Spenser strenuously manufac-
tures circularity through an elaborate stanzaic structure, including a
refrain which commands the outside world to duplicate the poem's
internal artifice. The cunning lustre of Spenser's poem, its strained
yoking of Catholic needs with Protestant stipulations, prevents any
moral evasions: every cosmic gap must be filled, every theological
chasm bridged. The music forced out of churches by Protestant
reformers now rings out in the streets, or is supplied at night by a
"Quyre of Frogs still croking" (1. 349).[27] And in place of Catholic
adornment, the poet-bridegroom offers his bride the fact that poetry provides its own compensations. A "Song made in lieu of many
ornaments" (1. 427), the *Epithalamion* itself is a "goodly ornament,/
And for short time an endlesse moniment" (ll. 431-33).[28]

In the sixteenth and seventeenth centuries, similar conceits about
poetry's grandeur or sheer appropriateness could also accommodate
the ambitions of witchcraft or the guarantees provided by a bur-
geoning London insurance industry. There was a new sense that
rhyming or arithmetic might redress natural disasters or replace
antique forms.[29] In Spenser's *Faerie Queene*, allegory provides another method, managing archaic thinking and organizing cultural artifacts by deliberately conflating symbolic foregrounds and back-
grounds. Shakespeare's stage likewise updates its medieval blue-
prints, redrawing ontological boundaries to provide places like the
black hole into which Hermione safely disappears for sixteen years,
or that allow the infidel Othello to "turn Turk" and die.
Shakespeare's contemporary Elizabeth Cary composes a play about
the rumors of a king's death to investigate more deeply royal origins and ends. Milton will give us in *Paradise Lost* an image of a past
to which we no longer have access, housed in an Eden now barri-

---

[26] An illuminating discussion of the Catholic rite is offered by Bossy (1989); see
also Lawrence Stone, *The Family, Sex and Marriage in England, 1500-1800*.

[27] See Jerome Mazzaro, *Transformations in the Renaissance English Lyric*. Mazzaro
mentions that reformers replaced music in the schools with arithmetic (95), a strategy Spenser seems to experiment with as well in his wedding poem.

[28] Edmund Spenser, *The Yale edition of the Shorter Poems*.

[29] See D. Keith Thomas, *Religion and the Decline of Magic: Studies in Popular Beliefs
in Sixteenth- and Seventeenth-Century England*.

caded from view. Their literary efforts are also necessary "translations of Christianity," as Bossy calls them, because they make its
ideas more powerful and accessible, shaping notions of the past no
longer organized by or indebted to sacred remains.[30] In the process,
literature's ambitions become more grandiose, and more satisfying.

***

My book challenges conventional readings of Renaissance culture as
an increasingly secular one. I propose instead that secularism is better construed as yet another method for interpreting the sacred.
Reformation theology required a radically different interpretive
framework to hold in place sacred meanings and values; such meanings had been shaken by a "discursive crisis" which occurred,
Thomas Greene claims, when Catholic ways of knowing were disrupted and its symbols dislodged.[31] Renaissance literature might
therefore be approached in terms of a sacred history of lost ideas,
and read in terms of sacred signs which were downplayed or even
disowned. Escaping the order imposed by theology, politics, or aesthetics, these sacred relics are no longer closely regulated, and a
number of "boundary" figures begin to linger at imaginative limits
or haunt cognitive thresholds.[32] I argue that these remains frequently cloud Protestant thinking and disturb its motives, the way
Hamlet's father's ghost hovers near purgatory, or the way purgatory continues to take up room even after it is officially shut down by
Henry VIII.

More broadly, the book is a study of "historical semiotics"[33] or
what theologian Jaroslav Pelikan terms "comparative symbolics,"[34]
focusing on beliefs or ideas that became outmoded but nonetheless
continued to influence Renaissance philosophy, geography, politics,
and theology. Of course, symbols create an environment which

---

[30] Bossy (1989) 152.

[31] For two accounts of what Greene calls a "discursive crisis," see his "Ritual
and Text in the Renaissance" (179-97), and "Post-Feudal Rhetoric and Historical
Semiotics" (46-56).

[32] See Harry Berger Jr.'s discussion of specifically literary—and typically conventional—boundary figures in "The Discarding of Malbecco." Such figures might
be found to inhabit the utopic regions Jeffrey Knapp describes in *An Empire Nowhere*.

[33] See Greene (1986).

[34] Jaroslav Pelikan, *Reformation of Church and Dogma 1300-1700* (2).

insists they ceaselessly remake themselves so as to remain timeless. Even during the sixteenth century, Arthurian legends served to legitimate dynastic claims, while the gradually weakened "threat" of Islam increasingly helped to consolidate the Western world. Another set of imaginative relics were produced when Catholic doctrines were repudiated and ideas about saints, purgatory or transubstantiation actively forgotten. Protestant theology–and with it, authors like Shakespeare, Spenser, and Milton–not only justifies but repairs these sacred losses.

***

An outline of each chapter provides a set of broken images or relics which together inspire Protestant theology. Chapter one explores how Reformation debates surrounding biblical apocrypha find their way into Spenser's *Faerie Queene*. There are few scholarly treatments of Renaissance apocrypha because early-modern culture is usually explored in terms of degrees of secularization; that there are consequent degrees of sanctity is precisely what Spenser's poetics calculate.[35] His poem furnishes an apocryphal account of Arthurian legend that supplements and corrects the canonical version with an undocumented story about the Prince's obscure boyhood. The chapter also examines the emergence of a new machinery for culture in the printing press. This apparatus provided additional techniques for memory and for forgetting, gradually allowing the popular image of the Turks to replace the waning symbol of Arthur and set cultural and political norms.

In chapter two, I explore how the Renaissance moral imagination was revised with the abolition of purgatory in 1534. Protestant iconoclasm must also be viewed as an historiographical practice, since rejecting purgatory inspired new paradigms for human history and new limits for human experience.[36] In the same way, Spenser's *Faerie Queene* invents romance sites where transcendence

---

[35] Kenneth Gross's study of idolatry and iconoclasm in *Spenserian Poetics: Idolatry, Iconoclasm & Magic* is an exception, although Gross does not take up Reformation debates on biblical apocrypha.

[36] See Ernest B. Gilman, *Iconoclasm and Poetry in the English Reformation: Down Went Dagon*; Duffy (1992); and David Loewenstein, *Milton and the Drama of History: Historical Vision, Iconoclasm and the Literary Imagination*.

can yield to philosophizing, when the sacred is temporarily pushed aside or disabled.

Similar tensions or collisions between history and theology are examined in my third chapter. I propose that Eve's recurrent displacements in *Paradise Lost* mirror Milton's ambivalence about his Hebrew sources. Created after the rest of Eden is finished, Eve is both supplement and obstacle, buried prize and secondhand fiction; exactly what she contributes to human history, or where she fits in, is not only unclear but contradictory in Milton's poem. Yet another contest which surfaces whenever Eve reappears in *Paradise Lost* is between past and present, and Eve's ambiguous status also reflects Renaissance anxieties over just which cultural memories ought to be repressed, and where they might be buried. This concern had arisen too when Hebrew materials, including midrash and other rabbinical commentaries, were recovered in order to shape a more authoritative scripture.

The first part of the book, chapters 1-3 ("Broken Idols"), concentrates on vacant cultural spaces (like purgatory or Spenser's faeryland) and abandoned icons (like Eve or King Arthur) to trace a widening gap between secular and sacred life, between poetry and belief. Chapters 4 and 5, which comprise part two ("Lost Causes"), investigate the eschatological implications of this gap, the ways that history is progressively disentangled from memory and nostalgia severed from experience.

I explore this nostalgia and the imaginative relief it can provide in my fourth chapter, where I examine Elizabeth Cary's *Tragedy of Mariam, The Fair Queen of Jewry* (1613). The first original play (we know of) written in English by a woman, *Mariam* considers the fate of tyrannical imaginations which believe themselves beyond history, a sentiment sometimes shared by Renaissance scholars who supposed that, in recovering the classics, they could recuperate a past somehow free of the present. Cary is especially interested in this presumption, I believe, because she herself chose conversion to (rather than from) Catholicism after Protestant reform.

The final chapter further examines the pressures imaginative relics exert by analyzing Hamlet's inability to avenge his father and bury his king. I argue that the same ontological difficulties are behind Reformation polemic surrounding transubstantiation, the Catholic belief that Christ's body and blood were actually present at the eucharistic sacrifice of the Mass. I trace the implications of

this crumbling eucharistic doctrine for patriarchal bodies, especially when Protestants convert the eucharistic feast to a mnemonic
device that, like the dislocated ghost of Hamlet's father, now only
signals itself.

In nearly every chapter I refer as well to a number of visual
images–frontispieces, altarpieces, and illustrations from the Polyglot
bible–as by-products or accidental signs invented in the course of
manufacturing Protestant doctrine or outlining belief. Although
Ernst Panofsky claimed that iconoclasm required sacred images be
abandoned altogether, not all symbols were completely destroyed.[37]
There were occasional efforts to retain visual images even while
pronouncing their artificiality. Spenser's self-conscious allegory provides only one way to skirt iconoclastic anxieties, since images had
both to do more and do less in the Reformation universe. The visual images assembled here record elusive or even disappearing
objects–purgatorial thresholds, temple ornaments, apocryphal texts,
transusbstantiated hosts–images that have yielded their rhetorical
power or been emptied of symbolic weight, yet somehow still manage to retain their shape. These indelible images not only illustrate
the eclipse of sacred signs, but depict the rebirth of the imagination
as a field for myth, superstition, and religion.

Throughout these pages I also view the scholarly construction of
"Renaissance secularism" as a particularly strained oxymoron,
unnecessarily obscuring, rather heedless of and strangely insensitive
to many aims and effects of Renaissance poetry. At the least, some
of the emotional investments Catholicism made were projected onto
the physical space offered by the New World, if initially as a site for
their failure or loss, as when purgatorial trials are relocated in
Virginia at Roanoke. Other environmental consequences are found
nearer to home, however. They are marked by the residue of stories and bodies which pile up when purgatory is abolished and transubstantiation revoked, the apocrypha isolated and the devil turned
Pope.

The persuasiveness of such residue may help us better understand the early-modern redefinition of the term "pathological."
Formerly characterizing illness, even plant disease, "pathology" now
comes to center around descriptions of moral susceptibility. As I

<hr />

[37] Ernst Panofsky, "Comments on Art and Reformation." *Symbols in
Transformation: Iconographic Themes at the Time of the Reformation.*

explore in my conclusion, one solution to the ravages of reform is the "arithmetic of memory" Hamlet bequeaths, which teaches us how to read discarded signs or failed symbols and take stock of the continuing power of dead or missing things. Hamlet's arithmetic partly replaces the "spiritual life insurance" that pardons once had granted.[38] But this book also suggests that a Renaissance "mortuary poetics" emerges by its side, proposing to view reality as something also constituted by a persuasive set of symbols. These poetics intimate that it is not heaven but reality which envelops us, a huge if empty landscape with its own hidden snares and traps, a new world that both requires science and commands belief.

---

[38] The analogy belongs to Clark-Maxwell, who further claims that much like insurance agents, pardoners worked under royal license. See "Some Letters of Confraternity" (49).

PART ONE

BROKEN IDOLS

CHAPTER ONE

TERMINAL HISTORIES AND ARTHURIAN
SOLUTIONS

Introduction

My project begins with a story of the apocalypse. In the spring of
1665, Jewish merchants were issued two instructions by an aspiring
rabbi named Sabbatai Sevi: they were told, first, to close their
accounts with English traders and, then, to unroof their houses in
preparation for a return to Jerusalem.[1] So striking in these directions is the unusual planning needed behind such a rupture or radical denouement. Why would old habits now appear fatally flawed
and old communities no longer possible to imagine? What catastrophe would require both the end of accounting and the demoli-
tion of ceilings?

Certainly, as Rudolf Hirsch reports in *Printing, Selling, and Reading
1450-1550*, the growing number of readers fostered by the mechanism of print was followed by a greater awareness of printers' errors
and faulty texts.[2] Old stories were not only found insufficient but
sometimes misleading, as Erasmus suggests when he complained
about the "contaminated, mutilated, lacerated and generally bad
texts" flooding the market more than a century earlier in 1528. The
solutions to this cognitive emergency were simple, if stark. One
might either choose to stop reading, or–like the Jewish merchants
told to drown history and narrative at once–to stop keeping count
and simply begin all over again.

But another solution was offered by literature itself, as a medium

---

[1] John Evelyn, *The History of Sabatai Sevi, The Suppos'd Messiah of the Jews* (71). See
also Christopher Grose's introduction (ii).
[2] See Rudolf Hirsch, *Printing, Selling, and Reading 1450-1550* (48); and John N.
Wall, Jr., "The Reformation in England and the Typographical Revolution: 'By
this printing . . . the doctrine of the Gospel soundeth to all nations.' " Describing
the effects of print on the Reformation, Wall argues that "what might otherwise
have remained a purely academic debate could become a more popular movement" (209).

into which readers' hopes might be dissolved or stirred. When
Renaissance scholars republished materials that had gone unread
for centuries, they unwittingly introduced a gap in knowledge, a
division between belief and authority. With the invention of the
printing press, this gap opened wider, betraying a discrepancy
between what could be known and what was read, what stories
could be told and what kind of thinking could be thought. Into this
chasm other data might get lost, like the accounts of English traders
or the apocryphal texts now pushed aside in the production of a
Protestant bible. Both readers and publishers seemed to be aware
of these possible losses, at least early on, and Hirsch notes that fully
half of the fifteenth-century book production consisted of reprints.[3]

A more intense, less manageable production of discrepancies
occurred with reports of current events circulated in pamphlets or
broadsides, the earliest newspapers. The German term for "newspaper" first appears in 1502, in a story describing Venetian struggles against the Turks.[4] This is especially noteworthy because the
Turk's image would continually be elaborated and sometimes dangerously multiplied in newspapers. Their reports enlarged the
"Turkish threat," making the end of the universe seem closer exactly at the moment when what constituted the universe could more
completely be known. Alert to such pressures, the early decades of
the Gutenberg era attempt to represent the Orient in a coherent
fashion[5] (long before the Renaissance theater aimed instead to split
its image apart). One early and avid reader commented in 1534:
"Nothing that is worthwhile to know, happens anywhere, that cannot be read in print";[6] and reading was almost synonymous with
reading about the Turks, popular culture a Turkish web.
Discovering one's own origins or connections was becoming
increasingly difficult, as the Jewish traders were told. This is what
Spenser's Arthur learns, too, when he uncovers a history on the
verge of collapse, finding his biography in Alma's Castle, a toppling
tower of Babel (2.9.21-22) housing narratives which only exclude
their readers.[7]

---

[3] Hirsch 83.
[4] See Kenneth M. Setton, "Lutheranism and the Turkish Peril" (137).
[5] See Douglas Brooks, "Orientals Like Us: Inexplicable Islam and the Staging
of the Orient in Elizabethan England" (unpublished essay).
[6] See Hirsch 151-52.
[7] See A. C. Hamilton's discussion of these connections in his edition of *The
Faerie Queene* (250-51).

The rejection of Arthurian legends Spenser chronicles in favor of the "eyewitness" accounts of the Turks newspapers provided, indicates a larger literary shift, from genealogy to narrative.[8] History now became textual material that could be usefully applied to a variety of stories, so that the apocalyptic apparatus of print proved helpful to Protestants who saw the pope–rather than the Turks–as the antichrist. The apparatus of print also bolstered the claims of sacred books by reminding readers of their own lateness or irrelevance. As a result, little support could be mustered against the Turks even when Greece was attacked and the origins of many Renaissance materials threatened. In fact, the Turks were seen as Trojan descendants whose victory merely represented long-deferred revenge against Greece.[9]

Both epic tradition and its romance alternative were emptied out by newspapers as their origins were recovered–made to resemble those houses without ceilings, unprotected and exposed when history was opened up to more urgent claims. As early as 1506, one pilgrim to Jerusalem noted the dimensions of this transformation: "All the countre of Troya is the Turkes owne countre by inherytance, and that countre is properly called nowe Turkey, and none other. Neuerthelasse he hath lately vsurped Grece, with many other countreys, and calleth them all Turkey."[10] What properly belonged to Turkey would keep changing, and only newspapers could track its constantly emptied boundaries.

The constantly disabled bounds of Renaissance history also explain some of the confusions surrounding Eumnestes, the figure of memory in Book 2 of Spenser's *Faerie Queene*. If the term *librarius* not only meant bookseller but denoted scribe, writing master or librarian,[11] Eumnestes stands for trader and reader, teacher and pupil, at once protecting and exposing knowledge that is both venerated and lost. Such an overburdened vehicle for history, Spenser proposes, can easily lose track of its sources. Spenser intimates too that there are just as many sophisticated techniques for Renaissance amnesia as there are for memory.

---

[8] Eisenstein 178, 303.

[9] See, for instance, Robert Schwoebel, *The Shadow of the Crescent: the Renaissance Image of the Turk (1453-1517)* (148); and Terence Spencer, "Turks and Trojans in the Renaissance."

[10] Spencer 332.

[11] Hirsch 61.

The rediscovery of classical materials invited the systematic displacement of other materials. At the same time, mass-produced
rumors about the ever-approaching Turks actually increased as the
distance from Turkish territory grew, suggesting the growth of
fiction as a source of knowledge, something more authoritative the
harder it was to verify. But these developments further suggested
that narratives of history could separate rather than unite a people,
and render one person unintelligible to another. Richard Helgerson
explores how print enabled the rise of imagined communities in
early-modern England–like the Protestant community John Foxe
celebrates in his *Book of Martyrs*. But Helgerson overlooks the fact
that such communities are almost always threatened or disappearing, perhaps because its members have nothing else left between
them.[12]

We might trace a history of reading, audiences, and subject matter in the Renaissance by exploring the widening divisions between
them. Printing created competing forms of knowledge along with
techniques to efface those differences, designing, for instance,
nationalistic typefaces that were both clearly recognizable and
sometimes impossible to read, or enabling the Church to issue
indulgences or formal remissions of sin.[13] Eventually extended to
liberate those trapped in purgatory, indulgences tried to bridge the
gap between worlds, to close an ontological discrepancy or make it
somehow manageable. Often they advertised more local threats, as
when indulgences called *turkenablasse* were sold in 1451 to relieve a
besieged Cyprus and absolve the sins of crusaders.[14] Hirsch reports
that indulgences were issued in greater numbers the further away
the threat of Turkish invasion, sold "not in territories where the
threat was greatest, but where the selling was most promising."[15]
One purgatory could loom large only when another seemed small;
and geography, politics, even catastrophe would from now on
depend on who was reading. As the Jewish traders believed, history might begin all over again after ending abruptly, for narratives
were portable and signs could be cashed in. The result was that

---

[12] Helgerson, *Forms of Nationhood: The Elizabethan Writing of England* (264-68, 284).
[13] Hirsch 9.
[14] See Schwoebel 166; and A.I. Doyle, et al., *Manuscript to Print: Tradition and Innovation in the Renaissance Book* (13).
[15] Hirsch 122-24.

what one did not know was replaced by a version of what could not be known.

***

We see this kind of replacement in Spenser's revelation in Book 2 canto 10 of *The Faerie Queene*. When Prince Arthur discovers the text of *Briton moniments* in Eumnestes' chamber (the seat of memory atop Alma's Castle) the scene is both a recognition and a reversal of his positioning in history—accounts are closed, and ceilings are razed. Typically embodying all of the virtues to which Spenser's knights aspire, the Arthur reading here becomes an empty symbol, because *Briton moniments* abruptly stops before naming him. The chronicle Arthur reads is a fractured history which fails to locate a legitimate origin, much like those Irish legends Spenser consulted to write his poem; both kinds of texts are apocryphal writings which interrupt history and displace national memory. Throughout *The Faerie Queene*, Spenser instructs his readers about English history by rewriting it, his allegory frequently breaking apart (as when the knight Guyon collapses in the middle of a canto or when the enraged Furor is literally stalked by his mother Occasion) to contemplate the sources, motives, even mechanics of the poem.

Spenser's practices are really no different from those at work in other projects of Renaissance historiography, which applied, collected or situated history as moral exemplum, classical precedent, sacred origin, or aesthetic ideal. The Renaissance past might thus be construed otherwise, shoved aside, downplayed or uprooted according to circumstance, even buried underneath the present in order to explain or justify it.[16] This also means that, as something created out of the present, the past could supplant or upset other actualities. Renaissance historiography actively invents ruins.

To be sure, our modern techniques of psychoanalysis posit only one way of recuperating the past, one that behavioralists would ignore as irrelevant or see as a cognitive obstacle. But what gets forgotten systematically in Renaissance texts is often still recorded by them as abandoned ends or romance alternatives. Ernest Renan

---

[16] See David Quint, "'Alexander the Pig': Shakespeare on History and Poetry;" and Nicholas Birns.

claims that not only remembering but "[f]orgetting . . . is a crucial factor in the creation of a nation."[17] Presented with their national epic, Spenser's readers are also given a set of false starts, faulty texts, failed experiments, and lame excuses, a history that must be pushed aside in order to forge a national consciousness. Such relics make up the faerylandscape of Spenser's poem, constituting a background ever alive to change, a history always reforming itself. Since he was exiled from Elizabeth's court, many of these relics were strewn for Spenser across Ireland. Milton will house such relics in Eden, so that they are permanently barred from us.

One of these relics is King Arthur, both historical source for *The Faerie Queene* and rhetorical possibility ultimately explained away by Spenser's poem. At the same time, as just one of many discarded signs or failed symbols, he remains useful to a Renaissance imagination not only prompted into existence by print but organized by its techniques for forgetting. If Eumnestes's chamber is a national museum which stores versions of history now obsolete, the Prince who studies his biography there becomes its most precious artifact and its most famous failure.

***

Sacred history has its store of exhausted artifacts as well, and Gershom Scholem describes one false start or failed experiment that offers a curious parallel to Spenser's account of Arthur. Relating the story I repeated at the opening of this chapter, Scholem explains how, in 1665–two years before *Paradise Lost*–a reluctant, melancholic kabbalist rabbi named Sabbatai Sevi was persuaded to reveal himself as the messiah. This announcement occurred only after his enthusiastic prophet Nathan of Gaza had, over the course of many months, convinced Sabbatai of his mission, most likely, Scholem claims, with the help of a Christian vocabulary and accompanying set of analogies. Sabbatai later told a follower that when Nathan originally cornered him, "[Sabbatai] laughed," acknowledging that "'I had [the messianic vocation], but have sent it away.'"[18]

---

[17] Ernst Renan, "What is a Nation?" (11).
[18] Gershom Scholem, *Sabbatai Sevi: The Mystical Messiah 1626-1676*; cited by Frances Yates in *The Occult Philosophy in the Elizabethan Age* (215-17).

Nathan's announcement generated enormous excitement in Jewish communities within Palestine as well as across Europe. Proclaimed sometime in late May of 1665, news of his announcement reached Europe by late fall of that year. A year later, however, Sabbatai disappointed his supporters when he apostatized to Islam. His believers, "perplexed because the messiah had taken neither the sultan's crown nor the crown of martyrdom,"[19] produced a variety of accounts to explain the disaster. Many describe the obvious, impossible choice between conversion or torture. But Christian accounts also proliferated, one gleefully announcing that Sabbatai had been awarded a purseful of silver. Another version, Scholem writes,

> [was] presented by the English consul in Smyrna, who had heard that Sabbatai replied with much chearfulness, that he was contented to turn Turk, and that it was not of force, but of choice, having been a long time desirous of so glorious a possession, he esteemed himself much honoured that he had an opportunity to owne it first in the presence of the Grand Signoir.[20]

An Armenian report pushed this scenario even harder, maintaining that "prolonged study of the Jewish writings had convinced [Sabbatai] of the truth of the Muslim religion to which he had secretly adhered for the last twenty years." Each proffered end could become a different beginning, while the end of history–at least the end of global history–was postponed for the time being. Finally, news about Sabbatai quieted down, and this particular dead end was absorbed by more pressing, if more local anxieties. Rarely is the apocalypse a global affair.

Two years later, Milton puts off the apocalypse in his own epic project to recover origins. "[L]ong choosing and beginning late," he picks unsung heroes over "tedious havoc" (*Paradise Lost* 9.26, 30), abandoning the story of Arthur for a narrative of "better fortitude" (9.31). Yet this substitution was something Spenser had earlier resolved upon, replacing the story of Arthur in *Briton monuments* with a second genealogy, the elfin chronicle Guyon reads. Never sure of the matter of Britain (Spenser rejects it entirely in his plans for Irish reform outlined in *A View of the Present State of Ireland*) he instead

---

[19] Scholem (1973) 694.
[20] Scholem (1973) 679-81.

occludes it here, so that Arthur's broken text adds itself to the long
list of ruptures which memory comprises in Eumnestes's "scrine."
Frequently the projects of nations or narratives bring together many
voices with the aim of drowning out individual ones. Yet Arthur
nonetheless seems an indispensable element to both. So why does
the Prince yield his messianic position in *The Faerie Queene*, ceasing
to allegorize England's destiny and become, instead, just another
stray piece of its history?

I believe this reversal is implicit in Spenser's poetic, and that
Spenser becomes Milton's "original" because Spenser so often for-
sakes origins. Repeatedly turning to non-canonical sources in order
to legitimate his political and literary projects, Spenser makes use of
Celtic legends, for example, to supply us with an apocryphal
account of Arthur's obscure boyhood.[21] As Frances Yates points out,
apocryphal writings, which conflated kabbalist and gnostic texts
with Christian, Pythagorean, Platonic, Neo-platonic and alchemical
works, supported the magician John Dee's imperialist labors,[22] so
Spenser was not alone in his efforts to link East and West, history
and pre-history. But Spenser appears less mystified than Dee (who
was, incidentally, nicknamed Merlin) or those Protestants who,
along with Archbishop Cranmer, rejected certain books as apocryphal when the Great Bible was issued, all the while employing a
self-consciously fictive Arthurian legend to legitimize Tudor claims
to the throne. If Spenser's method for inscribing national memory
often makes use of material publicly repressed, he at other times
rejects traditional common ground in order to bolster his imperial
epic. And, in contrast to Dee's mystical imperialism (or universalizing nationalism), Spenser in *A View* will promise his readers a separate volume on Irish antiquities.[23]

These habits might seem puzzling, but a comparable battle was
being waged in Protestant Europe at the same time over the fate of
apocryphal materials—those texts judged to be spurious or best kept
hidden, written too late, or in Greek rather than in Hebrew.

---

[21] Spenser's moderate Eudoxus maintains that the Irish bards' accounts are
"fabulous and forged," but the more severe Irenius insists that they can be used as
sources. See *A View of the Present State of England* (hereafter referred to as *A View*);
and Patricia Coughlan, "Ireland and Incivility in Spenser." *Spenser and Ireland: An
Interdisciplinary Perspective* (66-67).

[22] Yates 84, 95.

[23] See Judith Anderson, "The Antiquities of Fairyland and Ireland."

Apocryphal machinery (most popular in the Eastern branches of the ancient Christian church) appears designed to patch up canonical texts: one account supplies wives for patriarchs, another includes specific geographical place-names for biblical sites; others answer questions such as whether Adam and Eve produced daughters for their progeny. These texts tend, one scholar notes, "to carry back to Israel's early ancestors the institutions of culture" like writing, archaeology, and medicine.[24] In other words, this supplement is designed to make biblical history run more smoothly. But in the process, apocryphal materials often privilege history, as if under their rubric every sacred mystery could be brought to the market-place, something allegory (at least as its etymology suggests) was similarly designed to achieve.[25] Yet in the sixteenth century, the Great Bible (the bible of Spenser's boyhood) adds weight to its canonical claims by *omitting* apocryphal texts, and apocryphal books are labelled as such in the Matthew Bible.[26]

***

Another struggle for authority represented as an ambivalence surrounding its proper form is figured earlier in Book 2 of *The Faerie Queene*, where Medina (or "Equal") presides over a divided household containing her sisters Perissa ("Too much") and Elissa ("Too little") along with their lovers Hudibras and Sans Loi. Like Lear's three daughters, the sisters and their lovers convert this common ground into a battlefield (2.2.20). Eight cantos later, another seeming core is shown to be another false common ground. Arthur and Guyon are escorted to the top of Alma's Castle, where the mind is lodged and divided into three separate rooms. The third room,

---

[24] *The Interpreter's Bible* (1: 422-23).

[25] In his appendix to *Allegory: The Dynamics of an Ancient and Medieval Technique*, Jon Whitman explains how such rhetorical purposes are carried out by allegory.

[26] For a history of Renaissance treatments of apocrypha, see *The Interpreter's Bible, Vol. 1*. Interestingly, although the King James Bible (which includes the Apocrypha) has come to be recognized as the authorized version, no official action of authorization is known to exist (See 1:94).

Here and elsewhere my discussion is indebted to John Guillory (1983). Guillory describes how literature emerges when its inert relation to the Bible is disrupted (viii); Spenser and Milton thus displace the sacred in order to gain its authority and continue scripture. I use Guillory's model also to indicate how sacred texts might displace each other in similar fashion.

Eumnestes's chamber, is divided too, since he provides the knights
with two different chronicles of England. Throughout the knights'
tour of the Castle, David Lee Miller comments, one representational mode has repeatedly given way to another, so that the
"retractations of . . . anatomy . . . depend on erasures to frame
them."[27] This process occurs even within Eumnestes's chamber.
Miller supplies an explanation for these revisionary strategies: "In
the ongoing 'translation' of Western imperial culture" he writes,
"[t]he 'gentleman or noble person' Spenser seeks to fashion pursues
an ego ideal that would integrate the imperial self with an encyclopedia of its culture's symbolic paradigms . . . ."[28]

This consolidation (or recycling) of historical waste is also recorded in the text Arthur reads. *Briton moniments* is a collection of erup-
tions and breakthroughs, a history that proceeds or, really, collapses through a set of substitutions, dead ends, and paradigms that fail
to materialize. For one thing, we learn that England was from
"Celtike mayn-land brought," so that at its origins, the nation disappears to give way to hidden older claims, where "farre in land a
saluage nation dwelt,/ Of hideous Giants, and halfe beastly men,/
That neuer tasted grace, nor goodnesse felt,/ But like wild beastes
lurking in loathsome den, / And flying fast as Roebucke through
the fen,/ All naked without shame" (2.10.7.1-6). Indeed, the story
in *Briton moniments* is not one of imperial origins but of recessions
and invasions, inspired by vain illusion and driven by chance.
"[W]hence [these giants] sprong, or how they were begot,/ Vneath
is to assure," a tall tale, something ultimately even impossible to
believe.

When Arthur's biography abruptly stops before naming him, it
is replaced by Guyon's text, a smoother, steadier panegyric which
offers an alternative ontology to repair the Prince's faulty narrative.
The Elfin chronicles Guyon reads lack racial wars or irate Others
(like Saracens or Turks), and fashion a history which belongs to no
one. They absorb and correct Arthur's story, supplying him with a
different history—one that happens to someone else, over there,
abroad. Salman Rushdie would have us see this history as yet

---

[27] David Lee Miller, *The Poem's Two Bodies: The Poetics of the 1590 Faerie Queene*
(176, 178).
[28] Miller 73.

another paradigm of the culture, symbolic of the imperial self precisely because it does not replicate it.[29]

But why does Spenser replace Arthur's unconsciousness with a narrative of elf-consciousness? And why does the poet surround his failure to "nominate" Elizabeth with a "compensatory version" which makes use of a separate nationality, biology, and history?[30] By envisioning epic unconsciousness—or chronicling apocryphal history—Spenser eschews many ideas shared by sixteenth-century cartographers, legal theorists, and playwrights. Instead, he raises a question that must have perplexed the Jewish traders and many newspaper readers: What does it mean *not* to share a history?[31]

***

Indeed, this is a question Spenser will frequently pose. If nationalism, as Ernest Gellner writes, "is not the awakening of nations to self-consciousness [since] it *invents* nations where they do not exist,"[32] we are given a chance in Alma's Castle to study the kinds of narratives buried in the process. Elizabeth Bellamy suggests that "Renaissance epic history is really the story of how the unconscious *resists* interpellation into the ideology of epic."[33] We see this resistance in canto 10, when Arthur's "struggles against an emerging epic consciousness" are themselves represented and historicized. Arthur's mirror has changed into a screen on which these struggles might play out once more. Now serving as an imaginary origin, the Prince, in effect, becomes disposable.

But by borrowing Arthur from Ireland, Spenser sets the stage for his later rejection, since the Ireland described in *A View* is a founding text marked by incoherent syntax and illogical readings. Unlike Virgil's or Tasso's epics, which describe how the Eastern opposition ultimately falls apart again and again, the Western nation is repre-

---

[29] See Homi Bhabha, *The Location of Culture*.

[30] Elizabeth Bellamy poses this same question in "The Vocative and the Vocational: The Unreadability of Elizabeth in *The Faerie Queene*" (1, 5). See also Bellamy, *Translations of Power: Narcissism and the Unconscious in Epic History*.

[31] Both Benedict Anderson in *Imagined Communities: Reflections on the Origin and Spread of Nationalism* and Bhabha (1990) have raised the equally important opposite question: "What does it mean to share a history?"

[32] Ernest Gellner, *Thought and Change* (169); cited by Anderson 6.

[33] Bellamy (1992) 26.

sented by Spenser in *A View* as continually reconstituting itself, its
creation premised upon the "decreation" of cosmic order,[34] the era-
sure of sacred texts, and a production of anachronism. Spenser's
plans for Irish reform in *A View* insist on segregation, genocide, and
systematic forgetting. Not only must the land be emptied out
through drastic military action, but its history as well, and the
reform Spenser engineers an elaborate machinery designed to
release all of its weight.

Spenser even recommends changing volatile Irish surnames in a
scheme to develop a nomenclature for burying information. Irenius,
the "experienced Irish hand," calls for abandoning the names of
"septes" or clans: "from thenceforth each one should take vnto himself a severall surname eyther of his trade or facultie or of some
qualltie of his bodye or mynde . . . in shorte tyme learne quite to
forgette his Irish nation."[35] Just as he does by using the Elfin chronicles, Spenser turns Irish genealogy (both mnemonic device and
gauge of trauma) upside down and empties it out, like Arthur's
"bleeding wound" (1.9.7.3), so as to unload and disarm the past.

Still another method outlined in *A View* is to force history to
avert its gaze or to reject its subject matter, as when Spenser posits
earlier and earlier precedents for the Irish such as the Spanish or
the Africans.[36] But this happens too when epic Greeks are avenged
by Trojan descendants, or when Sabbatai Sevi turns messiah and
then turns Turk. *The Faerie Queene* works in this manner as well.
Commemorating the failures of the English Lord Deputy of Ireland
Arthur Grey, the poem is deliberately archaic or antique, addressing an audience now long dead (Perhaps for this reason Spenser can
so often put Prince Arthur to sleep).

A concurrent national project to relocate the meanings of the
past is described by Samuel Chew in *The Crescent and the Rose*, a
study of Islam and the Renaissance:

> The general notion was that Mohammedans were mere pagans,
> which explains the curious confusion in the *Chansons de Geste* between
> Saxons and Saracens and the fact that, as everyone knows, in old
> days the great rude monoliths of Stonehenge and other remnants of

---

[34] See Quint, "Epic and Empire"; and *Epic and Empire: Politics and Generic Form
from Virgil to Milton*.

[35] Spenser, *A View*. 201.

[36] Spenser, *A View*. 48-51, 57.

neolithic civilization in Britain were popularly known as Sarsen–that is Saracen–stones.[37]

The Renaissance image of the Turks had now shifted to register a set of unauthorized sources or inhuman forces. Yet the Turks' mis-shapen structures could effectively duplicate and reinforce the West's, as Reverend Joseph Hall alerted his readers in a 1607 epistle:

> when [the Turk] saw that he could not by single twists of heresy pull down the well-built walls of the Church, he winds them up all in one cable, to see if his cord of so many folds might happily prevail: raising up the wicked Mahomet, to deny, with Sabellius, the distinction of persons; with Arius, Christ's divinity; with Macedonius, the Deity of the Holy Ghost; with Sergius, two wills in Christ; with Marcion, Christ's suffering.[38]

Those who found themselves tempted by Islam would thus be seduced by something that promised to multiply its attractiveness because it could stand up to (or outside of) metaphor.[39] Viewed as a "synthesized culture," Islam was understood as a collection of apocryphal prophets and books accepted by no one, so that the text of the Koran best served to prove the superiority of Christianity over Judaism.[40]

Islam provided an endless supply of new discrepancies or transcendental signifiers, a chain of signs "always beyond the pale of representation."[41] In condemning the works of Catholics William Allen and Robert Bellarmine, Protestant reformer William Whitaker outlines a vital antagonism between a sacred tradition and those apocryphal elements it actively refuses:

---

[37] Samuel Chew, *The Crescent and the Rose: Islam and England during the Renaissance* (388). For an especially rich application of Chew's argument to Spenser's poetics, see Mark Heberle, "Pagans and Saracens in Spenser's *The Faerie Queene*."

[38] Rev. Joseph Hall, *Works* (1607) ed. Phillip Wynter (Oxford, 1863) vi; cited by Chew 445.

[39] Emily Bartels' *Spectacles of Strangeness: Imperialism, Alienation, and Marlowe* remarks on the multiplicity of Renaissance images of Turks without commenting on what appears to be their exponential value.

[40] See N.I. Matar, "Islam in Interregnum and Restoration England" (66). A century earlier, Pope Pius had described how the Turks "follow a certain false prophet called Mahomet, an Arab imbued with gentile error and Jewish perfidy." Schwoebel observes that the Pope saw Islam as "dedicated by its very nature to the overthrow of the Christian religion" (72).

[41] See Brooks (unpublished essay).

> For just as a dilapidated mansion, unless propped up almost every-
> day by fresh and firm buttresses, will suddenly fall in a violent and
> total ruin; so they perceived that the Roman synagogue, tottering as
> it is and threatening to fall, in its wretched state of decay and dilap-
> idation, hath need continually of new supports and bracings, to main-
> tain any remnant to its state and dignity under the pressure of such
> vehement assaults.[42]

Catholic accretions to scripture (the scaffolding of superstition
Milton will fault as "tradition" in *Paradise Lost*) here resemble the
support system Islam provided. In both cases, authority is guaranteed by the continued production of threats, and power ceaselessly
transmitted through the invention of new ends (see illustration 1).
This same powerful apparatus is at work in the New World slave
trade, where unknown others were brutally forced to justify and
substantiate outworn neoplatonic schemes.[43] It also underlies a
Renaissance hermeneutics that must keep addressing and bolstering
itself, a kind of knowledge that, like allegory, proposes to know a
world that is falling apart.

***

Some of the loudest tremors of collapse came with Sabbatai's
announcement and, then, with his apostasy. Spenser prevents such
a disaster by substituting for Arthur's broken text Guyon's elfin history. Print provides an ever-expanding teleology to organize or dis-
patch inconvenience, prohibiting the abrupt end of all connections.
We might even see both the faded threat of Islam and the worn
supremacy of Arthur as belonging to a complex set of catastrophes
or tropes now catalogued by the cultural machinery set into motion
by print. This machinery widely circulated a discredited genealogy
that allowed Henry VIII to trace his ancestry to Arthur through
"the irregular and wild Glendower," just as it permitted
Shakespeare's Hal to hear his secret adventures reported by "base
newsmongers" (see *1 Henry IV* 1.1.40; 3.2.25).[44] It is the existence of

---

[42] William Whitaker (1588) *Epistle Dedicatory* 4-5.
[43] See Elizabeth Mazzola, "Spenser and Slavery: Faeryland as Black Hole"
(unpublished essay).
[44] Also see Laurie A. Finke's discussion of such discredited genealogies in
"Spenser for Hire: Arthurian History as Cultural Capital in *The Faerie Queene*" (212).

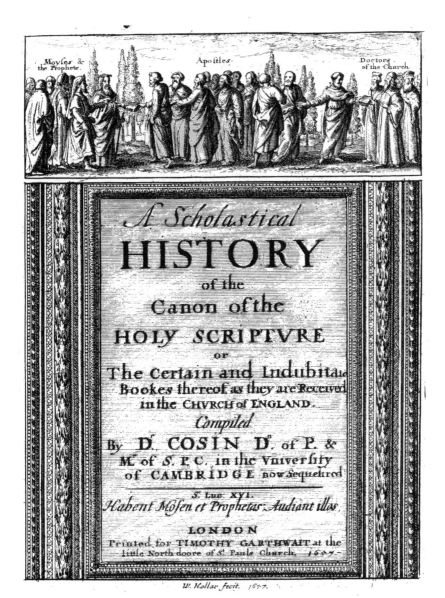

1. John Cosin, *A Scholastical History of the Canon of the Holy Scripture* (1657). At the top of the page is outlined a model of the perfect patriarchal transmission of texts and authority, a transmission that would seem to swallow the past whole.

such machinery that moreover forces John Evelyn–who provides our account of Sabbatai Sevi in his *History of Three late famous impostors* (1669)–to protect his own sources against the charge of "Imposture."

After Sabbatai was acknowledged as the messiah, of course, these discrepancies would finally come to an end. His followers had looked forward to that moment when "the Holy Temple should descend from Heaven already built, framed, and beautified, wherein they should offer sacrifice for ever."[45] Such an event was so crucial because it would mark the reversal of transcendental events, even if this reversal was something reproduced continually in "newspapers." But these reversals were also anticipated by Sabbatai's followers: Sabbatai's sovereignty was to be accompanied by an election of princes, where the priest Isaac Silvera would be renamed King David, and Elias Sevi given the title "king of the king of kings."[46] A letter dispatched by Jewish priests after the Sabbatai disaster only continues this trend. Fearful of the prophet Nathan's unabated enthusiasm, the priests warn foreign leaders not to succumb to transcendental pressures, reminding them that, after all, "[m]iracles are not to be Wrought every day."[47]

***

The priests teach us that history comprises those errors and relics and washed-up paradigms we are too ill-equipped to forget, the set of prejudices (and typefaces) print puts at our disposal. Edward Said suggests that this history, in turn, prevents us from endowing any one else with history, so that orientalism is "a system for *citing* works and authors."[48] The confusion it settles upon is figured in *A View* by the image of an Irish mother drinking the blood from her murdered son's head, in this way celebrating and draining his memory.[49] The grieving mother's example is doubled by the image of Arthur drinking at the fountain of memory in Book 2. As Tom Nairn suggests:

---

[45] Evelyn 48.
[46] Evelyn 64.
[47] Evelyn 106.
[48] Edward Said, *Orientalism* (23).
[49] Spenser, *A View* 81.

'Nationalism' [appears as] the pathology of modern developmental history, as inescapable as 'neurosis' in the individual, with much the same essential ambiguity attaching to it, a similar built-in capacity for descent into dementia, rooted in the dilemmas of helplessness thrust upon most of the world (the equivalent of infantilism for societies) and largely incurable.[50]

In a recent interview, Woody Allen mentioned an ever-pressing need to crawl back into the womb (anybody's womb), but most mothers and children, like nations and subjects, tend to be more selective. "No nation," Renan reminds us, "traces its origins back to Alexander the Great's momentous adventure, fertile though it was in consequences for the general history of civilization."[51] For the same reason, Spenser's faeryland is unable to serve as middle ground or home, a fact that takes its toll on each one of the knights. They frequently cannot identify each other immediately, and when they finally make some connection, spend most of their time catching up. As in Arthur's biography's abrupt ending, we read in these knights an "image of cultural authority . . . caught, uncertainly, in the act of 'composing' its powerful image."[52] Perhaps Spenser's belief that there is no center takes its toll on the poet too, but the Irish surely recognize Kilcoman to be his home when they burn it down.

Of course, singular epic gestures, like the one belonging to Spenser's Irish neighbors, are incoherent. But it is their failure or incoherence, like the withdrawal of Arthur, that marks the end of endings and allows empire to spread, forcing Milton (and Virgil and Tasso before him) to pull up the stakes and begin all over again.[53] Spenser helps us to see the mechanics up-close: in the course of his reading, Arthur has become as arcane as the rest of the materials in Eumnestes's scrine. Those are books that no one else is reading, their traumas limited to the Prince. But, then, we need to ask, when do its national myths start explaining Britain? If Troy was in the East, Spenser's Cleopolis is not England, so at what point does some

---

[50] Tom Nairn, *The Break-up of Britain* (359); cited by Anderson 5.

[51] Renan 9.

[52] Bhabha (1990) quotes Said's assertion that these acts consist of "subordination, fracturing, diffusing, reproducing," as much as of "producing, creating, forcing, grinding" (3-4).

[53] See Patricia Parker's discussion of the "westering" of empire in "Romance and Empire: Anachronistic *Cymbeline*."

Other begin explaining ourselves? Is it always at the beginning, as historian Martin Bernal emphatically suggests in *Black Athena* (an argument for the Afroasiatic roots of Western culture)?[54] At what point, however, do origins become so occulted that they "might as well not have existed"?[55] When Arthur, taken to be an origin for Elizabeth and Henry, is finally given an account of his origins, they fail to point to him.

This break in history occurred, too, when news of Sabbatai's apostasy circulated and allegory eroded the face of one of the gods.[56] Scholem's study of Jewish messianism explains the Sabbatai disaster in exactly this fashion. "No memories of a real person are at work here," he asserts,

> which, though they might arouse the imagination and attract old images of expectation, nonetheless are always bound to something deeply personal . . . [But t]his is just what the Jewish image of the Messiah, by its nature, cannot have since it can picture everything personal only in completely abstract fashion.[57]

Spenser's bleeding Arthur is the same kind of sign, emptying itself throughout the faerylandscape, an image that self-destructs, an allegory that simultaneously unravels and winds itself up. In this way *The Faerie Queene* makes room for Milton's aborted epic *The History of Britain* (1649-55), which concludes with the iconoclastic banning of Arthur altogether.

It would seem that only once the classical gods are resurrected can the "process of decay" be more decisively undertaken, and "a new, more authoritative structure of symbols emerge."[58] Spenser's allegory unveils a culture increasingly adept at multiplying meanings and systematically losing track of their implications. Its techniques belong to a literary category I would describe as a rhetoric of amnesia–a rhetoric Lear and Othello skillfully employ, painlessly dismantling authoritative symbols, tearing up a map of the kingdom or misplacing a cherished handkerchief from home.

---

[54] Martin Bernal, *Black Athena: The Afroasiatic Roots of Classical Civilization. The Fabrication of Ancient Greece 1785-1985. Vol. I.*

[55] This question is also raised by Birns, "The Trojan Myth: Postmodern Reverberations" (57-58).

[56] See Gordon Teskey, "Irony, Allegory, and Metaphysical Decay." (398).

[57] Scholem, *The Messianic Idea in Judaism and Other Essays on Jewish Spirituality* (17).

[58] See Teskey (1994) 404.

Spenser's solution makes Milton's choice that much easier. With so much Renaissance technology for nation, an original seems redundant, or obsolete.[59] The nation assumes its shape by reading not by remembering, and Arthur's private trauma can be converted to collective memory only when he is made to disappear, his personal suffering revised and amplified because he has been forgotten. Spenser's poetic thus opposes the therapeutic process, since his goal is to dismantle history in order that national identity might take shape.

Still, Freud's own archival impulses are well-known. He explains that "a child catches hold of . . . phylogenetic experience where his own experience fails him. He fills in the gaps in individual truth with pre-historic truth; he replaces occurrences in his own life by occurrences in the life of his ancestors."[60] If this practice is something Acrasia exploits in the Bower of Bliss, just as Freud saves memory by absolving it of pain Spenser saves history by cutting Arthur off from it.[61]

Conclusion

It is this rejection of an empirical ideal that, like the faery queen herself, is repeatedly embodied in *The Faerie Queene*. Arthur's wounds are psychological from the outset and his traumas strictly imaginary, so that rather than inaugurating epic consciousness, his chivalric behaviors actively and originally push it aside.[62] But the mechanism of print enables this kind of public forgetting as well, making possible the appearance of texts that would seem to compete with each other, like woodcuts that replace mutilated icons, apocryphal texts

---

[59] See Helgerson's (1992) revision of Greenblatt's notion of "self-fashioning." Helgerson describes the Elizabethan literary project to "remake the very cultural matrix in which [identities] had been formed" (25).

[60] Similarly, Teskey writes that "[a]uthority can be defined as the power to compel the public forgetting of what is privately remembered." See "Mutability, Genealogy, and the Authority of Forms" (108).

[61] See Robert May, "The Idea of History in Psychoanalysis: Freud and the 'Wolf-Man'" (175).

[62] Quint (1993) suggests that the East is typically positioned as the loser of imperial contests, only to be consoled by romance. Although Spenser is left out of Quint's important account, the poet does much to account for readers of epics, and explain why authors, continually "westering" empire, must keep beginning them over and over.

written prior to the saving word of the Gospel, and the "bogus
genealogies"[63] that now challenge epic origins. No wonder
Eumnestes relies so much on his assistant Anamnestes. But Spenser
also fills Eumnestes's chamber with machinery that substantiates literary history and synthesizes texts in face of the faults of which
Erasmus complained, here given form by Eumnestes' "feeble corse"
(2.9.55.6). It is this stable collection of broken signs, a "scrine" we
term "tradition," which permits the earth-shaking announcements
of false messiahs or true Turks. Printing authorizes not only what
Hirsch describes as the "complete secularization of the book,"[64] but
the complete secularization of crisis.

Preventing the community from imagining itself, Sabbatai Sevi
withdraws as a totalizing hero and it becomes necessary, for messianic culture to persist, to adhere to rabbinical commands to forget him.[65] Because he stands for both, Spenser's Arthur must also
be ignored as well, since the dreams of nation and of empire that
he "passes" for quietly conflict,[66] the battle staged at Alma's Castle
when parallel texts collide. But this collision almost goes unnoticed.
As Spenser tells us, the caretaker of these documents Eumnestes is
"halfe blind" (2.9.55.5).

---

[63] I borrow the term from Lawrence Stone, *The Crisis of the Aristocracy 1558-
1641.*

[64] Hirsch 1.

[65] See Scholem (1971) 95.

[66] For a carefully historicized account of this phenomenon, see *The Passing of
Arthur: New Essays in the Arthurian Tradition.*

CHAPTER TWO

EPIC LIMITS AND ROMANCE DETOURS:
NAVIGATING FAERYLAND

Introduction

Although abolished by Henry VIII in 1534, purgatory continued to
serve in the sixteenth and seventeenth centuries as an imaginative
holding ground or middle state, a romance alternative where epic
hopes could temporarily subside. Shakespeare keeps King Hamlet's
ghost stationed there in suspended animation while his son ponders
his own existence; purgatory may have no status within the
Protestant ethos and Prince Hamlet may be newly returned from
Wittenberg (Luther's home base), but how else to remind a son of
his practical obligations and familial responsibilities? The medieval
invention of purgatory characterized a universe more tolerant of
and responsive to men's errors or misgivings. The fiction functions
much like the mousetrap Hamlet sets, as a screen or place where
souls might be ensnared and their bad deeds finally come to light,
where history might repeat itself, but this time with a proper narrative behind it.[1]

Abolishing purgatory thus meant uprooting more than one set of
historical specimens and sacred remains. In getting to the "original"
Scripture, Luther had tried to bury most of the biblical arguments
bracing purgatory in books he labelled apocryphal and placed at the
end of the Old Testament.[2] But purgatory maintained a hold over

---

[1] As a university student at Wittenberg, Hamlet may be suspicious of the idea
of purgatory anyway. See Robert F. Fleissner, "*Hamlet* and *The Supplication of Souls*
Reconvened." Still, that purgatory addresses literary needs long after its theological usefulness is worn out is suggested by John Wooten, "From Purgatory to the
Paradise of Fools: Dante, Ariosto and Milton." Wooten notes: "*Paradise Lost* begins
in Hell, but shifts to Heaven without reference to Dante's middle kingdom *until*
Satan, on his way from Hell . . . reaches this midpoint location where a literary
allusion to Dante's Purgatory seems appropriate" (748).

[2] See Robert C. Denton's discussion of these books in *The Apocrypha, Bridge of
the Testaments: A Reader's Guide to the Apocryphal Books of the Old Testament*. Denton notes
that Second Maccabees "countenances the idea of the intercession of saints (15:14)

Renaissance imaginations, so that in order for its ritual activities to be discharged properly, the Shakespearean stage enclosed the tropes of heaven, hell and purgatory within its bounds.[3]

Although confining purgatory within the Globe would be one way to order a cosmos grown dangerously intractable, most Protestants' solution was simply to annul purgatory altogether and completely revise the ethical structures which elaborate cosmology. These structures, margins and boundaries which separate the sacred from the profane or the pure from the impure, guarantee unity against the magical tensions of disorder. The information about the universe these structures provide, as Mary Douglas argues in *Implicit Meanings*–information usually "treated as self-evident" and therefore never made explicit–furnishes the stable background on which more coherent meanings are based.[4] Just as the abominations of Leviticus, Douglas argues, remade the ground on which the Israelites could find order in the desert, the Reformation was undertaken with the sense that since the world is disorderly its map must be redrawn.

Douglas's description of epistemological boundaries uncovers the ethical pressures behind them, constantly at work to admit some experiences while excluding others.[5] There is a long history behind such mapping. In its Greek origins, political life or rule of justice was known as *kosmos* because as its rules changed, the cosmos changed as well.[6] Not only are "the laws of nature . . . dragged in to sanction the moral code;" Douglas suggests that "[t]he whole universe is harnessed to men's attempts to force one another into good citizenship."[7]

If this procedure is more complicated than one might think, it is because the universe proves more elusive than it appears. In fact,

---

and the practice of prayers for the dead, and could be quoted in support of the custom of offering requiem masses" (12:43-45) (19).

[3] In *The Idea of a Theater*, Francis Fergusson quotes George Riley Kernodle, *From Art to Theatre: Form and Convention in the Renaissance*: "More than an arrangement of side doors and inner and upper stages, that facade was itself a symbol of the castle, throne, triumphal arch, altar, tomb–in short, an all-purpose, eminently practicable setting, implying the constant elements in the Elizabethan world picture . . . " (116).

[4] Douglas (1991) 3.

[5] For an "ethnopsychological" account of religious geography, see Erich Isaac, "God's Acre" (29).

[6] Isaac, "Religious Geography and the Geography of Religion" (2).

[7] Douglas, *Purity and Danger: An Analysis of the Concepts of Pollution and Taboo* (3).

"[t]he sacred," Douglas claims, "is the universe in its dynamic aspect."[8] Edmund Spenser, whom Stephen Greenblatt describes as "one of the first English writers to have what we may call a field theory of culture,"[9] catalogs many of these dynamic aspects in *The Faerie Queene*. The poem's volatile romance cosmology is mapped as much by symbolic centers and sacred sites as it is by physical gaps and cavities, and organized by absences or dislocations like those following purgatory's shifting ethical weight. *The Faerie Queene* even suggests that oblivion has an ecology; and one of the poem's figures Phaedria goes so far as to recommend its attractions to the knights who visit her isle.

In this chapter I examine some of the cartographical and epistemological confusions diagrammed in *The Faerie Queene*. I also explore how places like Phaedria's refuge and purgatory not only attest to Renaissance romance's failure to offer an adequate ethical map, but improvise a solution. So often in Spenser's poem questions of ethos (moral choices involved in construing the world) are brought down to earth and encountered in the most pedestrian circumstances: navigating reality in faeryland involves moral bearing and physical orientation all at once. One example of the physicality of ethos–or morality of location–occurs when Arthur and Guyon read their respective biographies in Alma's Castle, as I explored in the previous chapter. Confined to an allegorical chamber of history installed within an image of the body, the two knights learn about the separate worlds they contain. But Phaedria supplies Guyon with a radically different set of directions.

***

When Guyon quits Phaedria's island at the end of Book 2 canto 6, he leaves the knight Cymochles behind, not thinking to rescue him. Later, Guyon will free Verdant and clear up the crowded bottle-

---

[8] Douglas (1991) xv.

[9] According to Greenblatt (1980), Spenser's "field theory of culture" conceives a nation "not simply as an institutional structure or a common race, but as a complex network of beliefs, folk customs, forms of dress, kinship relations, religious mythology, aesthetic norms, and specialized modes of production" (187). This chapter seeks to uncover how some of these "specialized modes of production" fashion institutional structures.

neck of romance in the Bower of Bliss. But his solution to the temptation Phaedria poses is simply to ignore it altogether:

> But he was wise, and warie of her will,
> And euer held his hand vpon his hart:
> Yet would not seeme so rude, and thewed ill,
> As to despise so courteous seeming part,
> That gentle Ladie did to him impart,
> But fairely tempring fond desire subdewd,
> And euer her desired to depart. (6.26.1-7)

The knightly dilemma created by Phaedria's lure of ease and tran-
quility greatly resembles Guyon's solution, his own form of courte-
ous oblivion that allows him to steer clear of her offer.[10] Guyon's
method for ignoring something seems useful but, when employed by
Phaedria, suspect and disturbing. There are, however, many other
strategies for ignoring something. Certainly Guyon appears rather
absent-minded in neglecting to bring Cymochles with him. This
other method, as Douglas maintains, involves suppressing information, pushing it to the background where it collects in unnoticed
channels of meanings or unexamined assumptions. Douglas claims
that in the "elusive exchange between explicit and implicit meanings a perceived-to-be regular universe establishes itself precarious-
ly, shifts, topples and sets itself up again."[11] In canto 6, Guyon's
ethos–his courtly customs–constitute the geography of this "regular
universe."

Another strategy for ignoring something is implicit in the pro-
tracted nature of Guyon's quest itself. As far as Phaedria is concerned, the only meaning of such a prolonged journey must be that
the "regular universe" is actually less perceptible than Douglas, at
least, suggests. For similar reasons, the rites of passage undertaken
in smaller or earlier societies have been revised for us through more
drawn-out procedures.[12] Instead of performing a sequence of dis-

---

[10] For a treatment of the courtly qualities of Guyon's resistance to Phaedria's
temptation, see William V. Nestrick, "Notable Prosopopeias: Phaedria and
Cymochles."

[11] Douglas (1991) 4.

[12] Arnold Van Gennep suggests that, especially for modern man, "[t]ransactions
from group to group and from one social situation to the next are looked on as
implicit in the very fact of existence, so that a man's life comes to be made up of
a succession of stages with similar ends and beginnings: birth, social puberty, marriage, fatherhood, advancement to a higher class, occupational specialization, and
death." See *The Rites of Passage*.

crete acts for a limited time in a designated place, we tend to undergo change gradually and in isolation: change now belongs to a more continuous pattern of abstraction of the individual from his or her society. Geography can even dictate ethos in these cases, and Spenser's knights, like Guyon or Calidore or Redcrosse Knight, continue their quests by withdrawing from them. It is when Redcrosse visits the House of Holiness that he discovers how utterly disconnected is his saintly destiny from his knightly adventures.

As Phaedria cannot help but notice, ethical dilemmas and destinations are not clear-cut in Spenser's poem. If the knights' movement across faeryland always seems to have a specific itinerary–announced in the proem or resolved upon within the first canto–what seems like a virtuous quest for transcendence at the same time becomes an effort to locate it. Their itinerary also requires rejecting earlier models of virtuous experience as sheer tropes of ethos, variously termed, Harold Bloom proposes, "fate," "destiny," "necessity," "experience," "limitation" or "nature."[13] Faeryland becomes more and more cluttered with those tropes as the poem continues. More places are registered as off-limits, rendered disenchanted, or forgotten about.

Given the diminishing geography of Spenser's poem, it is increasingly difficult to determine exactly what Guyon is doing in Book 2, avoiding or courting temptation, initiating himself in faeryland or protecting himself from its dangers. His journeying around faeryland differs from Redcrosse's trip in Book 1, because it seems more haphazard and is marked by fewer sacred sites. Critics like Lewis H. Miller and A.S.P. Woodhouse have claimed that Guyon's quest unfolds in a much more secular world, where there is less to read and more to see.[14] Graham Hough likewise comments: "The scene

---

[13] Harold Bloom supplies a list of such tropes in *Wallace Stevens: The Poems of Our Climate* (4-5).

[14] A.S.P. Woodhouse sets out to characterize: "Book I moves . . . on the religious level, or . . . with reference to the order of grace, and the remaining books . . . on the natural level only." As a result, "while the motivation and sanctions of the Redcrosse Knight's virtue are specifically religious, those of Guyon's just as clearly, are not. See "Nature and Grace in *The Faerie Queene*" (198). While Woodhouse characterizes the secular world, Lauren Silberman specifies its limits in claiming that Book 2 eschews many standard interpretive schemes: "Book II furnishes a critique . . . the object of which . . . is not so much Temperance itself, but the misappropriation of the classical virtue as a ready-made theoretical framework for acting in the fallen world." See Silberman, "*The Faerie Queene*, Book II and the Limitations of Temperance" (9). See also "A Secular Reading of *The Faerie*

of action is always the world, the temptations are those of ordinary earthly experience, and the means by which they are overcome are not revelation and grace but reason and self-command." Hough adds that "this very simplicity leads . . . if not to a moral ambiguity at least to an uncertainty about where some of the imagery is leading us."[15] Sometimes this uncertainty is also morally ambiguous. Many of Guyon's actions perform a strange synthesis of initiations and penances, as when he washes the blood from Ruddymane's hands or spends three days and nights in the underworld of Mammon's factory, deprived of food or rest. Apparently the sacred motives of Guyon's journey are still operative in Book 2, but, as Hough notes, the methods there appear uncertain and the destinations obscured.

More problematic, though, is what happens when Guyon goes off the beaten track in canto 6, when Phaedria lures him to her island and he interrupts his journey to Acrasia's Bower in order to briefly undertake another one. If Guyon appears more like a tourist than a Christian knight in Book 2, this particular stopover implies that geography has failed to specify an ethical system, and is unable to map sacred destinations or connect the kingdoms of Heaven and Hell. A map is missing in Book 2; instead, a "discontinuous, patchy space of practical paths" emerges.[16] The geography of Book 2 provides a method for tracking mistakes and confusions, impatience and black holes. Much of Guyon's journey might even be drawn as a chain of Bermuda triangles.

***

Phaedria's isle nonetheless locates a distinct problem. One might read her temptation of Guyon, often linked with the more sensual temptations of Mammon or Acrasia, as offering an incentive not to

---

Queene, Book II," where Lewis H. Miller, Jr. argues that in Book 2 "Spenser establishes [a] humanistic, non-sacramental ethic" (207).

[15] Graham Hough, *A Preface to The Faerie Queene* (154).

[16] Pierre Bourdieu suggests that: "By distributing *guide-marks* (ceremonies and tasks) along a continuous line, one turns them into *dividing marks* united in a relation of simple succession, thereby creating *ex nihilo* the question of the intervals and correspondences between points which are no longer topologically but metrically equivalent." See *Outline of a Theory of Practice* (105). Bourdieu is describing a system for the retrieval and dissemination of information, but it is important to remember that medieval maps did not always aim at accuracy.

abandon the quest but to allegorize indefinitely, not to keep going beyond, but merely to keep going on. Phaedria presents her world as a comfortable pastoral setting to which a knight might retire precisely because that world does not reward chivalric pursuits. She charms the sleeping Cymochles, her first victim, with this lullaby:

> Why then does thou, O man, that of them all,
> Art Lord, and eke of nature Soueraine,
> Wilfully make thy selfe a wretched thrall,
> And wast thy ioyous houres in needlesse paine,
> Seeking for daunger and aduentures vaine?
> What bootes it all to haue, and nothing vse?
> (6.17.1-6)

To be sure, as valiantly as the knights aspire, faeryland is indifferent and unresponsive. It almost seems an improper testing ground because there rarely is a winner. One way of redressing faeryland's failure to measure experience (either justly or promptly) lies in choosing a more fitting ground, but that kind of replacement—like the provisions of purgatory I take up a bit later—is a strictly-temporary solution. But Phaedria is not alone in recommending a newer, better romance locale that would improve on older models. This solution also explains why Gloriana first sends Redcrosse out on a knightly journey in order to prove he's a knight.

Bloom's collection of tropes is part of a larger discussion of Wallace Stevens, a poet who promotes many of Phaedria's own romance objectives. In a reading of Stevens' "Idea of Order at Key West," Bloom notes that Stevens' repeated use of the word "beyond" denotes a visionary, romantic impulse to transcend to a place like the realm of Shelley's skylark, "too high to be seen, with its song so acute or keen that it barely can be heard."[17]

The connections between Phaedria's song and the one Rinaldo hears in *Gerusalemme Liberata*, or even that performed by Keats' Belle Dame, have long been noticed by critics. Less commented upon are the striking correspondences between Stevens' poem and Phaedria's lyric. Both poems feature a lone female figure singing to herself, luring her listeners into a dangerous reverie. When Cymochles first sees her, Phaedria is:

---

[17] Bloom (1977) 98, 102.

> Making sweet solace to her selfe alone;
> Sometimes she sung, as loud as larke in aire,
> Sometimes she laught, that nigh her breth was gone,
> Yet was there not with her else any one,
> That might to her moue cause of meriment: (6.3.2-6)

Neither Phaedria nor Stevens' singer are attractive figures of temptation. They seduce their victims away from them into alienation and withdrawal, so that Cymochles, who "of his way had no souenaunce," abandons his quest altogether (6.8.3). In Stevens' poem, the singer gestures to her listeners not to sing with her but against her so as to create a world of experience which accommodates no other experience. After Stevens' narrator and his companion listen to her song, the narrator tells us:

> Then we,
> As we beheld her striding there alone,
> Knew that there never was a world for her
> Except the one she sang and, singing, made.[18]

Transcendence becomes identical with invisibility, where tropes of ethos cease to work rather than are surpassed. As Bloom puts it, Stevens "affirms a transcendental poetic spirit yet cannot locate it."[19]

Such movements "beyond" in *The Faerie Queene* traverse less sufficient worlds of experience. Guyon simply moves from Phaedria's island to Mammon's cave, and then from Alma's Castle to Acrasia's Bower. Ethical categories in *The Faerie Queene* are thus diffused and at the same time rendered more concrete. And, while Spenser implicitly raises the question of whether experience can ever be free of a world, Stevens instead asks whether the world can ever be free of experience. Such questions themselves are posed differently within psychological and sociological realms of ethos. For Bloom, *ethos* takes its meaning from the Greek "limitation," so that success at love or poetry becomes a matter of evading or limiting limitation. But like the Greek *nomos* or law based upon a division of land,[20] ethos originally meant a habituated place; only since Heraklitos and Aristotle has it been associated with the "character"

---

[18] *The Palm at the End of the Mind. Selected Poems and a Play.*
[19] Bloom (1977) 104.
[20] Issac (1964-65) 30.

of a person or culture. Individual experience for Bloom takes its shape by ignoring a conceptual geography or distrusting empirical evidence. Douglas's (1970) definition of ethos, in contrast, requires acknowledging and systematizing such a conceptual geography in place of the dissolved personal ties and obligations which delineate the local ritual world. In either case, what Bloom and Douglas both suggest is that a poverty—an actual if sometimes imaginative need for new symbolic forms or actions in a local or limited ethos—provokes some kind of compensatory action, one that might also involve advancing to new settings.

This compensation is provided by the continuation of the poem after the apocalypse is postponed in Book 1. Both Woodhouse and Lauren Silberman have explored how this continuation enacts a movement from a sacred to a secular realm. Contrary to Douglas's argument about the universalizing of experience in such a movement, Guyon's path is distinct from Redcrosse's because it seems to unfold in a wholly earthly and much more limited world.[21] The ability to read and decipher is less crucial in this world than it was in Book 1. More important is a kind of readiness and good timing. In addition, less strength and concentration is needed by Guyon simply to enter or leave what C.S. Lewis terms the "allegorical cores"[22] or what Northrop Frye calls the "houses of recognition" in the poem.[23]

At Phaedria's island, though, Guyon only briefly tolerates her off-color tales and jokes, gets increasingly irritated and, after a skir-

---

[21] While Book 1 is marked by a proliferation of sacred and profane sites, there is in Book 2 a glut of other models of experience. Silberman argues, for instance, that in canto 2 the palmer's explanation of original sin as the cause of Ruddymane's bloody hands is inappropriate and ineffective in a primarily secular world, while the fountain Guyon stops before in order to clean Ruddymane's hands has a moral history itself, as a shrine to a maiden who refused to yield her virginity (11). Silberman further maintains that in Book 2 "the typological pattern of sin and redemption" is replaced by "mediating earthly experience." She adds: "Typological allegory saves the world of appearances from being merely transitory and phenomenal, but it offers little help in contending with the phenomena of the physical world. The problem of actually coping with fallenness, or mediating, rather than transcending, earthly experience is deferred beyond the conclusion of Book 1" (10). Still, the necessities or limitations explored within Books 1 and 2 both require a relation to the world: secularism does not merely connote any relation to the world, but a particular one. In other words, the itineraries in Books 1 and 2 are different and not subsumed by each other.

[22] C. S. Lewis, *The Allegory of Love: A Study in Medieval Tradition.*

[23] Northrop Frye, *Fables of Identity, Studies in Poetic Mythology* (77).

mish with Cymochles, demands to be brought back to the shore
where Phaedria had originally found him. She quickly grants his
wish, somewhat irritated herself (6.37). It seems that Phaedria's
island is less an "allegorical core" of the poem and more a mistake
or accident which, unlike Acrasia's temptation to a "self-contained
world of experience," composes no world at all.[24] In some ways,
William V. Nestrick notes, "Guyon is saved from Phaedria by his
taste: when her merrymaking passes the bounds of modesty, deco-
rum becomes a reality principle, not an aesthetic one."[25] Guyon's
stop there halfway in Book 2 and halfway to the Bower of Bliss[26]
requires a reader to rethink the critical mapping of the poem from
"temple" to "labyrinth" or from sacred to profane. Like Mammon's
and Acrasia's realms, Phaedria's island is an abstraction, but unlike
them it is an inadvertent one, just as at times experience without
effort becomes image or sensation, as thought breaks off, emotion
runs dry, or weariness or boredom interposes itself. In effect,
Phaedria makes such accidental experiences the only experiences.

Indeed, Phaedria's realm fashions itself out of the premise of
those kinds of accidents and mistakes, out of the threat that experience might free itself entirely from the world. Maleger stands as a
later example of this threat, brought back to life in canto 11 each
time he has been struck down by Arthur. Guyon's faint in canto 8
signalled another, although the angel who attends him appears to
protect Guyon from this particular consequence. Phaedria most
clearly embodies the threat. Nowhere in the poem does Spenser's
allegory ever fully shut down; instead, Phaedria proposes to take the
knights out of circulation for awhile, providing them not with
rewards or pleasures but merely with an opportunity to sleep. Her
world is a "second world" derived from the poverty of the faerylandscape: its inability to supply clear directions to Gloriana's court
or provide rewards or sanctuaries, except accidental ones.[27]

***

[24] See Michael Oakeshott, *Experience and its Modes* (331). The particular dilemma is that the ethos of Phaedria's isle recognizes no competing ethos, so her world
then provides the only location for viewing the world. Cf. Nestrick, who argues
that Phaedria "sets up independent microcosms, worlds that lack certain connections but that frame an abstract and brief epitome of all that is most pleasant in
nature" (61).
[25] Nestrick 68.
[26] Harry Berger, Jr., *The Allegorical Temper: Vision and Reality in Book II of Spenser's
Faerie Queene* (227).
[27] Derived from the poverty of imaginative experience, such a second world

In romance, these second (and sometimes third or fourth) worlds are not always versions of an original paradise but purely temporary realms, places which appear and then more quickly disappear from view. Occasionally, these places erupt merely out of the failure of the romance ethos to image something more than a peculiarly technical arrangement of adventures. The fragility of the connection between first and second worlds is thematized in a species of romance featured in early Celtic legends known as *imrama*, which depict a sea voyage across a chain of temporary islands, each island more material than the one before.[28] Many Celtic legends involve this motif, in which a hero accompanied by a few companions wanders about from one island to another and encounters fabulous adventures everywhere.

The earliest and most famous legend is the seventh-century *Imram Brain*, which chronicles the adventures of Bran and his men in the land of women (Emne).[29] The story begins with Bran who, after having fallen asleep one day, awakens to find an apple branch by his side. He brings it to the fairy court, where an unearthly female visitor reveals that Bran will make a journey to Emne. Bran and his company depart for the island, but they first visit the Isle of

---

stands in contrast to Berger's description of the Renaissance "second world" as a "playground, laboratory, theater, or battlefield of the mind . . . . Its essential quality is that it is an explicitly fictional, artificial, or hypothetical world. It presents itself to us as a game which, like all games, is to be taken with dead seriousness while it is going on . . . . Separating itself from the casual and confused region of everyday existence, it promises a clarified image of the world it replaces." See *Second World and Green World. Studies in Renaissance Fiction-Making* (11-12).

[28] In Appendix 7, Volume 2 of the Variorum edition of Spenser's *Works*, "Celtic Elements in Book II," Edwin Greenlaw discusses the Celtic *imrama* with particular reference to the Mammon and Acrasia episodes. Greenlaw also cites W.F. Thrall's proposal that Celtic *imrama* derived from the *Aeneid*. See Thrall, "Virgil's *Aeneid* and the Irish *Imrama*." Thrall claims, however, that while Irish scholars of the sixth and seventh centuries might have had access to and been familiar with the classical tradition, *imrama* primarily make use of native material (66). Other scholars have argued for a Celtic precursor to Dante.

[29] My text of *Imram Brain* is edited by Kuno Meyer, *Imram Brain, The Voyage of Bran, son of Febel, to the Land of the Living; an old Irish saga, now first edited, with translation, notes, and glossary (1895-97)*. In the afterward, Alfred Nutt argues that the latest *Brain* manuscripts belong to the sixteenth century, so Spenser indeed may have been familiar with the story; for one thing, as other critics often note, Spenser's description of the Bower of Bliss bears a remarkable resemblance to the Celtic Elysium *Mag Mell*, described by a female visitor to Bran's court, who reports that it is: "Without grief, without sorrow, without death,/ Without any sickness, without debility." Furthermore, at *Mag Mell* there is an arbor of gold leaves, and beneath it, "A beautiful game, most delightful/ They play (sitting) at the luxurious vine,/ Men and women under a bush,/ Without sin, without crime."

Joy where a member of Bran's crew insists upon staying. They leave him there and proceed, finally reaching Emne, an idyllic place luxuriously supplied with several beds for each pair of lovers. The men remain for hundreds of years, although it seems to them just a year. Finally, homesickness overtakes them and they resolve to leave Emne. Before departing, however, Bran's men are warned by the Queen of the island not to touch the shore of their homeland. They set sail for home, but as they reach the coast one of Bran's crew jumps overboard, races to the shore and, upon reaching it, turns instantly into a heap of ashes. Bran and his men are forced to tell the story of their voyage to the descendants of their kin from their boat in the sea.

The relative continuity of time and space preserved throughout most of Guyon's trip in Book 2 clashes markedly with the *Brain* legend. Guyon, returning from Mammon's cave, only faints; moreover, the sense that he has lived through an experience is attested by the change in environs and not obscured by it. When romance is spatialized in the *Brain* legend and transcendence becomes a location, the metaphor of experience as journey breaks down. Spenser's Phaedria has a similar goal. She tries to entertain her visitors with lewd tales and jokes, turning "all her pleasaunce to a scoffing game" (6.6) and trivializing the romance yearnings of the knights. In contrast to the beautiful maiden in Celtic lore who warns the visitors to her island of the perils of returning home, Phaedria simply asks Guyon why he left home in the first place.

What in *Imram Brain* becomes the romantic image of the visionary lost at sea appealed no doubt to Coleridge's picture of the Ancient Mariner, just as it does to Phaedria, for whom tropes always seem more forceful somewhere else. It is for this reason that she denies Guyon's initial request to depart, telling him:

> Who fares on sea, may not commaund his way,
> Ne wind and weather at his pleasure call:
> The sea is wide, and easie for to stray;
> The wind vnstable, and doth neuer stay.
> (6.23.2-6)

Nevertheless, if Phaedria's world arises out of the degeneration of "custom" and "necessity" and "fate," at the same time it is beautifully and compellingly staged:

No tree, whose braunches did not brauely spring;
No braunch, whereon a fine bird did not sit:
No bird, but did her shrill notes sweetly sing;
No song but did containe a louely dit:
Trees, braunches, birds, and songs were framed fit,
For to allure fraile mind to careless ease.
(6.13.1-6)

In Stevens' revision of canto 6, the singer exerts herself much more than Phaedria does, inventing the world alongside of which she sings and simultaneously saving that world from any experience of ethos:

She sang beyond the genius of the sea
The water never formed to mind or voice.

and yet its mimic motion
Made constant cry, caused constantly a cry,
That was not ours although we understood,
Inhuman, of the veritable ocean.

The untranslatable–or unethical–quality of the singer's experience somehow increases the expressiveness of her song, so that the narrator exclaims "[i]t was her voice that made/The sky acutest at its vanishing." But if they fade in Stevens' poem, the transparent pressures of reality, according to Phaedria, only provide a reason to escape reality. Pointing to "[t]he flowres, the fields, and all that pleasant growes," she argues

they themselues doe thine ensample make,
Whiles nothing enuious nature them forth throwes
Out of her fruitfull lap; how, no man knowes
They spring, they bud, they blossome fresh and faire,
And deck the world with their rich pompous showes;
Yet no man for them taketh paines or care,
Yet no man to them can his carefulle paines compare.
(6.15.3-9)

Phaedria thus offers an experience in which the world would drop out, as all tropes of ethos are exhausted rather than transcended.

The ease with which Phaedria erects a philosophical haven out of faeryland makes faeryland itself seem like a dream. It appears empty to her because it is cluttered with indecipherable meanings. Commenting on how Phaedria tropes the Sermon on the Mount,

Nestrick claims "what is wonderful and amazing about her agnostic vision ('how, no man knowes/ They spring') is the seeming lack of causality" in nature,[30] encouraging Phaedria to invoke nature itself to justify limitation and necessity. Harry Berger, Jr. compares this episode to Guyon's encounter with Mammon two cantos later: "where Phaedria wants man to believe he is all body, Mammon tries to make him forget his body and concentrate on the goods of the spirit."[31] But Phaedria discards more images than Mammon does. In her world, nature is no longer a ground but a trope; and she urges the knights to relax by removing the site for rest. Early-modern colonialism would similarly rewrite the ground for moralizing so that tropes of ethos were rendered increasingly mechanical and abstraction violently deliberate. This substitution soon occurs within Spenser's poem, however. Once Guyon escapes Phaedria's isle, Cymochles' brother Pyrochles, now enraged and sick with passion, jumps into a lake screaming "I burne, I burne, I burne," (6.44.1):

> Perdie, then is it fit for me (said he)
> That am, I weene, most wretched man aliue,
> Burning in flames, yet no flames can I see,
> And dying daily, daily yet reuiue: (6.6.1-4),

It is as if Pyrochles' own limits or nature simply has become too painful for him.

***

More ambitious than Phaedria's agenda, Spenser's treatise on Ireland entitled *A View of the Present State of Ireland* (written in 1596, but issued after his death in 1633) asserts that the English settlement there would flourish only through the extermination of the Irish. Ireland was not simply another culture in Spenser's tract but another world, where "England's law, culture and religion had been exposed as the most delicate of organisms."[32] In these environs, Celtic *imrama* would empty out England as well. But Ireland pro-

---

[30] Nestrick 66.
[31] Berger (1957) 226.
[32] Ciaran Brady, "Spenser's Irish Crisis: Humanism and Experience in the 1590s" (41-42).

vided merely one location for such magical transactions. During the sixteenth and seventeenth centuries, iconoclastic debates raged in England and across Europe, and paintings, statues and other sacred images were destroyed by "the enemies of idolatry."[33] Like the English colonists, Protestant reformers insisted upon the creation of a horizontal ethical space that sometimes ruthlessly excluded other values. Eventually Queen Elizabeth's own portrait was dragged through the mud.[34]

Their ethos, shared by Phaedria, is duplicated by emerging anthropological interests which reflected colonial impulses to retain old values upon the ruins of the new. Even the developing Renaissance interest in "individuality," as Greenblatt explains, coincides with a need to institutionalize it:

> It has been traditional, since Jakob Burkhardt, to trace the origins of autonomous individuality to the Renaissance, but . . . individual identity in the early modern period served less as a final goal than as a way station on the road to firm and decisive identification with normative structures.[35]

According to Claude Levi-Strauss, early-modern imperialism is organized by the same methods:

> The historical conditions of that development which was to benefit the Western world were brought together by the destruction first of the New World itself . . . . This destruction enabled the development to happen in the first place, before it could return to impose itself from the outside on the very societies it had destroyed in order for it to be born and grow from their ruins.[36]

More's *Utopia* could be added to this list of new ruins. Richard Helgerson describes utopia as a good place or no place "which supposes no miraculous transformation of either nature or human nature." He accounts for its genesis in terms of a "secular trust of negation."[37]

---

[33] Gilman 1; and John Phillips, *The Reformation of Images, Destruction of Art in England. 1535-1660* (121).

[34] Phillips 121.

[35] Stephen Greenblatt, *Shakespearean Negotiations: The Circulation of Social Energy in Renaissance England* (75).

[36] Claude Levi-Strauss, *Structural Anthropology*, Vol. 2. (316).

[37] Richard Helgerson explores colonialism as a response to the deterioration of the European world, but like Levi-Strauss he suggests that by "putting the sign of

We might explain the early-modern fascination with unusual cultural artifacts in terms of this context, as well. The sixteenth-century curio cabinets described by Margaret T. Hodgson and Steven Mullaney demonstrate an interest in material values construed as "new" because they had ceased to have any instrumentality.[38] Emptied and perceived in this way, the second world would quickly become a concept, its time and space immediately subsumed by the viewer's own ethos. We witness Hamlet's father confined in purgatory, reminding his son of his own familial reservations and wishes, and urging him from a supernatural realm not to forget the laws of kinship. Attending to the ghost's request not to forget him, Hamlet is finally absorbed by an antique cosmos, and in his success ultimately turns the crown over to the more archaic standard-bearer Fortinbras.

***

Hamlet's father's ghost substantiates a cosmology which Phaedria herself tries to specify, one which might make the loss of meaning itself symbolic. Her aims differ from those New Historicist interpretative practices which would invest this loss with symbolic plenitude. For example, in describing how Renaissance theatrical entertainments provided to the lower classes filled a void created when "[p]opular and liturgical forms were appropriated by the secular authorities [and] . . . transformed into exclusive celebrations of the monarchy or urban elite," Louis Montrose raises the specter of a world increasingly bereft of its own tropes of custom, necessity, and fate. "Unlike so many ritual and ceremonial forms of pre-Reformation culture," he argues, "Elizabethan symbols of power did not address the tangible concerns of ordinary citizens, transient workers, or the huge, subordinated groups of youth and women."[39]

---

negation on the world they knew, men opened the way to another world. Much of the subsequent history of the West has been a response to that opening—whether an attempt to shut it off and reaffirm the order it called in question or to occupy and inhabit it." See "Inventing Noplace: Or, The Power of Negative Thinking" (102-03).

[38] Margaret T. Hodgson, *Early Anthropology in the Sixteenth and Seventeenth Centuries*; and Steven Mullaney, "Strange Things, Gross Terms, Curious Customs: The Rehearsal of Cultures in the Late Renaissance."

[39] Louis Adrian Montrose, "The Purpose of Playing: Reflections on a Shakespearean Anthropology."

Montrose wonders: "What symbolic forms accommodated the problems that daily life posed to them?"[40] An even-more pressing question might be: What symbolic forms accommodated their loss of symbolic forms, especially when this loss was so widespread? After all, one cannot read the poverty of symbolic forms as necessarily meaningful. The artifacts arrayed in curio cabinets were valued because they were not instrumental, because they did not promote understanding. In parodying the Sermon on the Mount, Phaedria actually recommends this kind of reading to Guyon:

> The lilly, Ladie of the flowring field,
> The Flowre-deluce, her louely Paramoure,
> Bid thee to them thy fruitlesse labours yield,
> And soone leaue off this toylesome wearie stoure;
> Loe loe how braue she decks her bounteous boure,
> With silken curtens and gold couerlets
> Therein to shroud her sumptuous Belamoure,
> Yet neither spinnes nor cardes, ne cares nor frets,
> But to her mother Nature all her care she lets.
> (6.16)

Phaedria's impulse is not only replicated in the co-opting of symbols by high culture but in the iconoclastic banning of sacred images by official ecclesiastic culture. The two movements are closely-entwined, as John Phillips suggests, noting that the new interest in other cultures frequently derived from a need to replace "unsafe" with "safe" imagery:

> All sorts of symbolic ornaments came to be carved on tombs. Indians, skulls and crossbones, scythes, urns, weeping cherubs holding doused torches were substituted in place of the traditional Christian symbols that were every day being destroyed. These changes of a conceptual nature suggest not a progress from religious to secular representation; rather, the character of traditional Catholic imagery gave way to a new religious imagery devoid of traditional identifications and hence safe.[41]

Reformation iconoclasm revises both the art-historical and anthropological philosophies of the period. It belongs to an ethos which, perhaps for the first time, perceives art as produced by art, by

---

[40] Montrose 59.
[41] Phillips 118.

human labor, plans and alterations and subject thereby to human codes of substitution and revision. As part of such a system, it becomes clear that sacred images have to be replaced rather than abandoned altogether.

Because of the necessity of substitution, it would be a mistake simply to read secularism into iconoclastic impulses or locate it behind other forms of religious experience which during the Reformation–or, for that matter, at any other time–disappear, are forced underground, or are projected somewhere else.[42] Secularism may characterize a method for directing impulses. It is not the cause of such projections.

***

In fact, we might read purgatory as a new place clearly designed to handle old impulses. In *The Birth of Purgatory*, Jacques Le Goff describes the creation of this third world between heaven and hell as the "domestication of the next world."[43] Arguing that purgatory's function was primarily secular rather than theological, Le Goff finds an economic motive behind its creation, fostering indulgences which allowed the building of churches and hospitals while lessening the suffering of the dead. "What an enchantment of the power of the living there was in this hold over the dead!" Le Goff argues. "Meanwhile, here below, the extension of communal ties into the other world enhanced the solidarity of families, religious organizations, and confraternities."[44]

According to the Catholic Church's justification of the concept, however (articulated, Le Goff maintains, no earlier than the twelfth century–the era of romances and Avalon and the monks' discovery of Arthur's body at Glastonbury),[45] purgatory was not a thruway

---

[42] See Douglas (1970) who, with the purpose of exploring the varied reserves of symbolism in modern life, writes that: "Seculari[s]ation is often treated as a modern trend, attributable to the growth of cities or to the prestige of science, or just to the breakdown of social forms. But [secularism] . . . is an age-old cosmo-logical type, a product of a definable social experience, which need have nothing to do with urban life or modern science. The contrast of secular with religious has nothing whatever to do with the contrast of modern with theoretical or primitive. The idea that primitive man is by nature deeply religious is nonsense" (ix).

[43] Le Goff 213.

[44] Le Goff 12.

[45] Le Goff also claims the "success of Purgatory was contemporary with the rise

that would improve the conditions of the two worlds it connected but a separate arena which spatialized ecclesiastic doctrines of justice. "Although the doctrine of purgatory is not explicitly stated in the Bible, belief in its existence is intimately related to the Biblical doctrines of divine judgment, the forgiveness of sins, the mercy of God, and the temporal punishment due to sin." Indeed, this newest addition to the cosmological order was taken to be the most self-evident by English recusant William Cardinal Allen (1565), who questions whether "because of lacke of space, or late recociliation of the offender, shall oure lorde of necessity be forced to remit the debt, and release his sentence of justice for lacke of meanes to pounishe in an other worlde?"[46] Since it would be heresy to suggest either that God's justice had limits or that it did not take into account men's limits, the existence of purgatory frees both God and his worshippers from ignorance. This is something John Floyd (1613) testifies to, maintaining "we were from Paganisme conuerted to the Catholick beliefe of Purgatorie; yea that S. Gregory whome your Mynisters use to charge to haue bene the greatest Patron of this doctrine, was the chiefest Author vnder God of this our happy purgation from heathenish superstition."[47]

Le Goff's investigation makes clear what Celtic *imrama* had long insisted, that the universe is magically ordered and reordered by men's journeys. The twelfth-century vision of Tnugdal recounted by Le Goff specifies, for instance, that

> while the geography of the other world is still fragmented, with Hell as such appearing to be unified because it cannot be visited, three principles are begging to govern the organization of various purgatorial places. The first of these is geographical: we pass from one area to another, the transition being marked by the contrasts of terrain and temperature. The second is moral: those undergoing purgation are distributed among the various places according to the nature of their vices. The third is, properly speaking, the religious, not to say theological: men are [now] classified into . . . categories.[48]

***

of the narrative. More than that, the two phenomena are related. Purgatory introduced a plot into the story of individual salvation. Most important of all, the plot continued after death" (291).

[46] William Allen, *A Defense and Declaration of the Catholike Churchies Doctrine Touching Purgatory* (33).
[47] John Floyd, *Purgatories Triumph over Hell* (1613).
[48] Le Goff 191.

Perhaps another symptom of purgatory's vast ethical weight or cognitive power is the degree to which it had been relatively ignored
as an imaginative setting prior to Le Goff's analysis. While historians have recovered countless traces of sacred images and paintings
consigned to reforming flames, literary critics and historians have
tended to leave purgatory out of catalogs of other worlds (especially if they omit hell). One critic explains, "I have . . . limited my
investigations to the longed-for country . . . and have therefore
excluded the places of torture and punishment . . . [which are] left
out of account because in general [they have] little to do with the
mysterious, enchanted, or delightful regions we are examining in
romance and allegory."[49] He implies, too, that the introduction of
a third realm like purgatory might indicate that the world was not
perceived as sufficient for experience (see illustration 2). But
Catholic recusants repeatedly explained that a sinner's being condemned to purgatory resulted from his failure to carry out an ethical itinerary which had already been scheduled. Allen, for instance,
insists: "This was Paules rule, that if we woulde pounishe or iudge
our selves, then woulde not God iudge us."[50]

Prior to the 1530s, disbelief in purgatory was confined to the
Lollards. Even their criticisms were intermittent though, compared
to the charges more typically levelled against them, like

> scoffing at pilgrimages . . . denying the efficacy of holy water and
> holy bread . . . possessing the scriptures and devotional works in
> English . . . . From such dissenters might emanate criticism of the
> abuses of the chantry system and occasional unsystematic attacks
> upon purgatory itself. A full-scale onslaught against the doctrine of
> purgatory, however, would require a new theological mainspring
> which would go far beyond the simple piety . . . and the 'popular
> materialist skepticism' of the Lollards.[51]

The Lollards' reluctance was also explained by the fact that repudiating purgatory, unlike banning sacred images, involved an impe-
tus for social reform which, at the same time, dismissed the contri-
butions of individual effort or pain.[52] Privileging ethos over ethics,
later Protestants would divide the two.

---

[49] See Howard Rollins Patch, *The Other World, According to Descriptions in Medieval Literature* (5).
[50] Allen 47.
[51] Alan Kreider, *English Chantries: The Road to Dissolution* (95-96).
[52] According to Kreider, John Foxe claimed in 1534 that from this time "'pur-

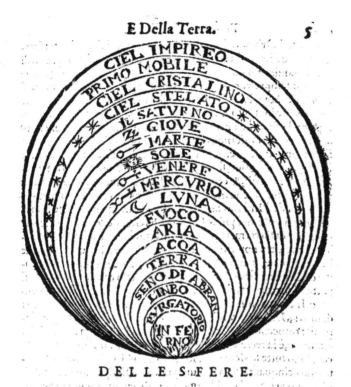

E Della Terra.　　　　5

DELLE SFERE.

G Iouanni di Sacrobofco, diuide la Sfera in due modi, vno fecondo la foftanza, & l'altro fecondo l'accidente. Secondo la
foftanza, in noue sfere: Nella nona sfera detto primo Mobile, nel
la sfera delle ftelle fiffe, che fi dice firmaméto. Et nelle fette sfere
de'pianeti; cioè, Saturno, Gioue, Marte, Sole, Venere, Mercurio, &
Luna: La foftáza, effentiale ftella fi dice: qual'è la piu defa parte
del Cielo, ò dalla forma sferica, che sfera chiamiamo, qual per la
fua denfità reflette a noi i raggi Solari, & quefti fono i pianeti lo
pradetti. Il firmaméto fi dice qllo, che porta le ftelle ferme, & fil-
fe in effe. Secódo l'accidente fi parte in sfera retta, obliqua; La ret
ta s'intende a quegli, che ftanno fotto l'Equinotio; perche fem-
pre hanno i Poli elfuati equidiftanti, tanto l'Artico, come l'An

A　3　　　tartico,

2. Giuseppe Rosaccio, *Teatro del Cielo e della Terra* (1595). Purgatory is depicted as just one of many circles which organize
the universe and cluster about hell. As part of such a system, its
existence is therefore inevitable, logical, necessary.

This shift can be illustrated by Henry's calculated attitude toward purgatory. The King's plans for dissolving the monasteries impelled him to reject it, a strategic decision having little in common with Luther's bald opinion that there was "no bigger lie on earth than purgatory."[53] Henry's consolidation of power after his split from Rome demonstrates that, at least in England, political emphasis was turned away from internal domestic disputes (where the chief concern was justice) to a focus on international affairs and the protection of boundaries (a concern with security).[54] This new emphasis resembles Mammon's itinerary which eclipses other worlds or Acrasia's aim to colonize all experience.[55] In contrast to Henry, Hugh Latimer will reject ethos altogether. Preaching in 1536 that "[t]he founding of monasteries argued purgatory to be; so the putting of them down argueith it not to be," Latimer repudiates the concept of purgatory rather than purgatory itself.[56]

Conclusion

Perhaps because of the largely political nature of Reformation struggles, "materialist skepticism" frequently fails to invade purgatory.[57] The purgatory finally rejected thus differs from romance destinations which are more quickly disposed of or routed off the map.

---

gatory & such trumpery began to grow in contempt.' [And] in spring of that year Archbishop Cranmer issued an order commanding all preachers to inveigh against the papacy and forbidding them to speak out in defense of purgatory" (104).

The repudiation of the "Romish Doctrine concerning Purgatory" was formulated as no. LXXII in the Thirty-Nine articles of Religion, first promulgated in the 1549 Prayer Book. See Theo Brown, *The Fate of the Dead, A Study in the Folk-Eschatology in the West Country after the Reformation* (15).

[53] See Kreider 94, 96. Luther's primary statement *Ein Widderruff vom Fegefeur* [A Recantation of Purgatory] (1530) is not available in English. A hand-copied Latin translation entitled *De Purgatorio* was dedicated to Henry VIII by Luther's associate Georg Spalatin (Kreider 137).

[54] See Norbert Elias, "State Formation and Civilization" in *The Civilizing Process*. Isaac's (1965) discussion of the historical replacement of ethical limits with national boundaries suggests why the repudiation of purgatory coincides with the production of national maps: "in order to liberate the world from the secularization which it bestowed, the church conducts a mission in it. This means that the church itself becomes secularized and acquires the paraphernalia of political institutions *in imitatio imperii per sacerdotium*" (10).

[55] Isaac (1965) 10.

[56] Phillips 41.

[57] Kreider 95-96.

These places are the residue of romance, fabulous other worlds now surpassed, overlooked or, like Phaedria's realm, spurned as accidental. In contrast, purgatory's existence continued in popular legend, in literature and within ethical systems long after its abolition by Protestant reformers. According to popular Celtic legend, for instance, a pit at Station Island in Ireland–rumored to have been shown to St. Patrick by Jesus–remained a site for pilgrims to experience purgatorial pains in life and so avoid them after death, at least until the early eighteenth century when it was shut down by the pope.[58] The other site now taken to be a location for purgatory was Sicily, Arthur's resting place.

Purgatory and Phaedria's island are other worlds which repudiate the goals and scene and ethos of romance, but both places nevertheless are romance sites, along with Avalon, the place where Arthur sleeps. Such places, *temporarily* inhabited (whether by Arthur, King Hamlet or the Irish pilgrims), result from the insufficiency of a system of ethics to provide clear directions to Heaven or to Hell, or to control individual experience through its wide array of tropes (see illustration 3). Frye describes the "refrigerated deathlessness" of the "most naive versions of romance" in comic strips, where "a central character who never develops or ages goes through one adventure after another until the author himself collapses."[59] In theory (and making the proper adjustments in climate), purgatory works along the same lines. Like Phaedria's island, where Guyon is briefly led in "immodest Merth" and "loose desire" away from the realization of his quest (see Book 2 proem), purgatory is a place where tropes of ethos cease to work rather than are surpassed, a place which accommodates the reduction of symbolic forms and does not replenish them. Continence is learned there, although not from the inside out (that is, by saying "no") but from the outside in (by experiencing external limits). Catherine of Genoa likewise described purgatory as a place whose ethical machinery was much more manageable than Hell's: in purgatory no resistance was put forward

---

[58] See the translation of *Tractatus de Purgatorio sancti Patricii* entitled *St. Patrick's Purgatory, A Twelfth-Century Tale of a Journey to the Other World*. Although its history was first compiled in the twelfth century, the site was reputedly established seven centuries earlier as a monastic retreat. Le Goff writes that, even now, "every year some 15,000 pilgrims visit the site between June 1 and August 15" (199). Le Goff also refers to the voyage of Bran (402 n48).

[59] Frye, *Anatomy of Criticism: Four Essays* (186).

3. Abraham von Karlstadt's *Sermon vom stand
der Christglaubigen Seelen* (1523). Here purgatory is not a world but occupies the space
between worlds; a threshold rather than a site,
purgatory is a place for transcendence whose
own boundaries are fluid, contingent, inde-
terminate.

since all of the conditions of experience appear provisional.[60] Both
the romance landscapes of purgatory and Idle Lake might be seen
not as pictures of transcendence but as the "pigeonholes of oblivion" Douglas describes.[61] They are places which draw new and crucial experiential distinctions that, at the same time, are not felt.
Spenser's hoggish Grille is therefore left behind at Acrasia's Bower
because he is as insensible to his condition as the "damned ghosts"
and "carkasses exanimate" which had clogged Guyon's and the
Palmer's passage there (2.12.6.5; 7.5).

Still, it seems more "realistic," emotionally as well as cognitively,
to subdivide the world and posit a place between Heaven and Hell
rather than to imagine nothing at all. Purgatory took up space that
already existed, and what made rejecting it even more complicated
than inventing it (whether in the twelfth century, or earlier, as
accounts of St. Patrick's purgatory attest) was the fact that purgatory does not represent an Eden. Rather, purgatory was a place
which explicitly ignores beginnings and transcendence. We might
even see the sixteenth-century's replacement of the future world of
purgatory with the adjacent world of America as conveniently substituting a geographical scheme of good and evil for a conceptual
one.

This same substitution is at work in Celtic *imrama*, where abstrac-
tions of reality crush imaginary ones, yielding a new romance site
which does not return us to an original situation or rediscover a lost
Eden. Instead, like the material islands in the *Imram Brain* or
Phaedria's isle, purgatory and More's *Utopia* are places of correction
where "two disjointed universes" are synthesized: "the violent and
irrational world of experience and the supernatural universe of
sacred principles."[62] When this synthesis is complete, the first world
is repudiated, although not for a more beautiful world but for a
more material one. This synthesis seems complete in Stevens'
Esthetique du Mal, where he deduces that "the greatest poverty is not
to live in a physical world."

A pragmatic analogue to Stevens' revision of romance is found
in the views of sixteenth-century iconoclasts and Protestant reform-

---

[60] *Purgation and Purgatory.*
[61] Douglas (1975) 4.
[62] Edward Schillebeeckx, O.P. and Boniface Willems, O.P., eds., *The Problem of Eschatology. Concilium: Theology in the Age of Renewal. Vol. 41* (155 n15).

ers. Before he had simply rejected the idea of purgatory outright, Luther had been admonished by the Catholic Church for claiming in 1489 that those in purgatory continue to sin insofar as they shrink from pain.[63] Luther insisted, that is, upon the same ethos for purgatory and earth, with the implication that the way to escape purgatory would be to ignore the symbols of its reality. Luther here teaches the colonizing of the romance world, a posture which, in turn, makes the repudiation of the New World that much easier.

If Spenser's pragmatism in *A View* belongs to a civil servant, it still seems often cruel, calling for widescale extermination, genocide, and the systematic forgetting of Irish history. In *The Faerie Queene*, his mood is more tempered, almost empathetic, since it frequently signals itself by withholding judgments. With the cancellation of Phaedria's isle, the rejection of Mammon's House, and the destruction of Acrasia's Bower, Guyon does not find himself finally installed in Gloriana's court but only stranded once again in faeryland. Depleted of those romance landmarks, faeryland has become something of a moral vacuum at the end of Book 2. Compared to the world at the close of Book 1, it is a place where no decisions can be made about fate, no rewards administered, no ceremonies celebrating the victories of virtue.[64]

At this point in *The Faerie Queene*, only Archimago appears occasionally successful at staging contests there, and Phaedria, perceiving the "therapeutic" value of such official rituals, tries to compensate for their loss with a distracting change of scenery. Paul Halmos's description of psychotherapy in *Solitude and Privacy* helps to distinguish her methods from other models of treatment:

> In many respects the ethical ideals of psycho-analytic therapy are reminiscent of Christian ideology which promises the Kingdom of Heaven as a reward for individual salvation instead of furthering the cause of an 'earthly Kingdom' first in which all would find their individual salvation. They are both individualist-perfectionist systems in which it is only the individual's sin or the individual's neurosis that matters . . . [W]hether it is sin or neurosis, the individual's escape

---

[63] *The New Catholic Encyclopedia* (1038).

[64] Patricia Parker thus states, "The Christian 'respite' in the wilderness before the Sabbath rest becomes, in the purgatorial space of 'faerie,' the interval of 'wandering' between vision and fulfillment, between the initiation of the quest and its end, in both senses." See *Inescapable Romance: Studies in the Poetics of a Mode* (59).

from these inflictions is to be made without even an attempt on the part of the healer to change the sufferer's environment.[65]

There is much to recommend Phaedria's island, and Guyon's strategy of refusal, his polite ignorance, postpones a real refusal. In this way, he also reserves judgment and preserves her realm. In later books of *The Faerie Queene*, when much of the narrative takes place under the sea, in a secret clearing in the forest, or in a temple, the poet has altered the environment and readers are presented with spectacles in which the knightly viewer imaginatively inserts himself (or herself), rather than places like purgatory or Phaedria's isle in which the participant will seek to absent himself. Especially in Books 5 and 6, Spenser attempts to project experience back onto a recognizable romance locale, much like Theseus does in Chaucer's *Knight's Tale*. But in later episodes of the poem, Spenser also calls into question the idea of a journey. As embodied by Arthur, Florimell, Calidore and Britomart, it more and more seems merely like fleeing, evading, shadowing or spying. Indeed, the quest finally collapses in a secret ritual, when Calidore thoughtlessly topples the hidden universe of which Cymochles, fast asleep, does not even pretend to dream.

---

[65] *Solitude and Privacy, A Study of Social Isolation, its Causes and Therapy* (128).

CHAPTER THREE

REFORMATION AND REPUDIATION IN
PARADISE LOST AND THE DIVORCE TRACTS

Introduction

Nothing was forever buried in Milton's imagination: outworn symbols became useful as typologies, fallen angels divine agents, lost paradises epic poems. One of his most strained images–which surfaces first in the divorce tracts–not only explains why Miltonic memory is so roomy but suggests the tremendous agony of its accommodations, especially when two symbols or figures are made to share the same status or carry the same weight. In this case, however, Milton is describing the tensions produced by a failed marriage. "[I]nstead of beeing one flesh," he writes, "husband and wife will be rather two carkasses chain'd unnaturally together; or as it may happ'n, a living soule bound to a dead corps."[1] This particular analogy, which strains to yoke together two different ontologies, becomes increasingly powerful in Milton's poetics, as when he combines Christian and pagan traditions.[2] But in this chapter I suggest that Milton's Eve offers another solution to such tensions. Appearing and disappearing repeatedly in *Paradise Lost*, she assumes a large part of the burden of poetry herself.

***

Many readers have viewed *Paradise Lost* as an ideal container for obsolete items. Isabel MacCaffrey argues that: "The uniqueness of *Paradise Lost* is in a sense its perfect victory over uniqueness; the very thoroughness with which Milton has assimilated the themes."[3] Part

---

[1] *Complete Prose Works of John Milton. Volume Two 1643-1648* (326). All references to Milton's divorce tracts are to this edition (abbreviated *CPW*) and will be cited parenthetically in the text.
[2] See Thomas N. Corns, "'Varnish on a Harlot's Cheek': John Milton and the Hierarchies of Secular and Divine Literature."
[3] Isabel Gamble MacCaffrey, *Paradise Lost as "Myth"* (2).

of the poem's success, MacCaffrey implies, derives from the obsolescence of its subject matter, for "when the myth . . . became irrelevant to the world's convictions, the poetic manner created to embody it became obsolete or, vainly applied to non-mythical subjects, extraneous and dead."[4] Another way to put it would be to call *Paradise Lost* an apocryphal text. Composed more than a thousand years after the sealing of the biblical canon, it is a less authentic, even spurious third testament, a narrative restricted to kabbalistic circles, of dubious importance and questionable authority.

To be sure, many poems might fall under such usage. This is because "apocrypha" usually designate a collection of biblical narratives authored not by scribes but by scholars, conceived of as literature, meant to repair institutional structures and canonical texts rather than supplement those traditional oral stories (the literal word of God) only accidentally preserved. Within *Paradise Lost* are buried other apocryphal stories: banned or hidden information to which we no longer have access, like Eden itself now barricaded from view, or simply the experience of Adam quietly laboring in the garden by himself while Eve converses with the snake. This is the other meaning of "apocrypha," signifying books set aside for the wise, but suggesting too a form of cultural detritus specifically excluded from providential schemes.

There are still other imaginative relics which continue to haunt the perimeter of Eden. Neither wholly inside or outside its borders, they include repudiated texts or shadowy figures like Milton's Hebrew sources or even Eve herself, which belong to sacred memory and at the same time interrupt it. Perhaps the categories of "sacred" and "secular" are inadequate to the complexities of Milton's narrative, as Mark Wollaeger argues, because *Paradise Lost* provides its readers with the chance to watch these sacred memories recede from view.[5]

***

Some of Shakespeare's relics work as antecedents for the images Milton withdraws. Just as Eve makes it possible for Adam to under-

---

[4] MacCaffrey 4.
[5] Mark A. Wollaeger, "Apocryphal Narration: Milton, Raphael, and the Book of Tobit" (148).

stand himself (perhaps she is such a good listener because she mir-
rors him so well),[6] Desdemona, shunted between father and husband, provides a similar service for Othello. In the same way Eve
manifests Adam's heart's desire, Desdemona reports that "I saw
Othello's visage in his mind" (1.3.252). Anticipating Milton's
emphasis on "rational burning" above carnal satisfaction, Othello
requests his new bride's company on their wedding night, "not/ To
please the palate of my appetite,/ Nor to comply with heat, the
young affects/ In my defunct, and proper satisfaction,/ But to be
free and bounteous of her mind" (1.3.261-65).[7]

Moreover, Milton's and Shakespeare's narratives are both constructed to place female characters outside, even though, ironically,
both figures are prized for their attentiveness. Maybe the frequent
connection between Iago and Milton's Satan is explained in contrast by the latitude each is given by the narrative. But Desdemona
and Eve are quickly repudiated and made obsolete by the stories
which surround them.[8] It might be Desdemona's pliancy which
finally proves her undoing, her genealogy which "unmoors" her; as

---

[6] As Marshall Grossman explains in "Servile/ Sterile/ Style: Milton and the
Question of Woman," "Prior to the creation of Eve, [Adam] is the one thing in
Eden that he cannot behold . . . he insists on another of his kind so as to make
himself visible to himself" (149).

[7] While these particular connections have not been previously noted, a number
of critics have linked the two works in other ways. James Grantham Turner suggests a different kind of analogy between *Othello* and *Paradise Lost*, claiming: "There
are quite simply two time-schemes [in both works] . . . . [Like Othello and
Desdemona] Adam and Eve are at the same time young lovers, tragically snatched
away after a few nights of love, and a mature couple." See *One Flesh: Paradisal
Marriage and Sexual Relations in the Age of Milton* (288). In *Pursuits of Happiness: The
Hollywood Comedy of Remarriage*, Stanley Cavell brings together Shakespearean
romances and Hollywood talkies to provide a model of conversation and explain
the relative success of second marriages in Hollywood films of the 1930s and 40s.
Milton's divorce tracts and Freud find their way into this extremely rich discussion.
The allusions may be more extensive than even Cavell implies, however; he points
out that in "The Philadelphia Story," Tracy Lord/ Katherine Hepburn is told by
her father that she "lacks an understanding heart" (137); in *The Doctrine and
Discipline of Divorce*, Milton evokes Solomon's "understanding heart" (Kings 1.3,
CPW 2:12). See Merritt Hughes' notes in *John Milton, Complete Poems and Major Prose*
(703 n44). All references to *Paradise Lost* are to this edition and will be cited parenthetically in the text.

[8] Even at the outset, both brides are prized for a modesty which almost renders them unfit for marriage. Absorbed by her image in the pool, Eve is initially
reluctant to yield to Adam's more solid form. Similarly, Desdemona is "So still and
quiet, that her motion/ Blush'd at her self," and upon learning of the nuptials,
Brabantio is skeptical that his daughter, "Against all rules of nature," could "fall
in love with what she fear'd look on" (1.3.95-98).

Othello angrily promises Lodovico, "she can turn, and turn, and yet go on" (4.1.249). Still, if Milton seems to come to the same conclusion about Eve in *Paradise Lost*, he ultimately reserves judgment. Much of the poem is organized instead around what to do with Eve, how and where to locate her, more obsessed with the power to evoke her and to put her to sleep again.

In fact, throughout *Paradise Lost*, Eve is continually recalled, never superseded. Like Othello's missing handkerchief, she consistently provides "ocular proof" (3.3.366) usefully testifying to many conflicting readings. Wollaeger reminds us that narratives continually generate their own secrets or "new opacities," but we should be alert both to the "temporal ironies" at play here and to a vastly expanding network of epistemological ironies as well.[9] They work differently from Spenser's discarded images and exposed optical illusions—like the Bower of Bliss or false Florimell, the abandoned hermaphrodite and even the absent body of Gloriana—which litter *The Faerie Queene*, so that something is always rotting in the state of faeryland. Instead, Milton's divorce tracts, like his epic, contain and even cultivate his ambivalence about marriage. To be sure, Renaissance culture frequently disowned cognitive stances, epistemological frameworks and ideological positions in order to shape a rhetorical construct we would call history. But in *Paradise Lost*, Milton calls this construct Eve.

***

> [S]he can turn, and turn, and yet go on,
> (*Othello* 4.1.249).

The same tensions Milton deals with in *Paradise Lost*, where he negotiates the awkward gap between the moral status of the past and its chronological positioning, are behind Brian Walton's *Biblio Sacra Polyglotta* (1654-57).[10] Walton's text arranged columns of scripture in nine languages (including Aramaic, Hebrew, Syriac, Chaldee and Greek) alongside the Vulgate, so that the Polyglot bible was not

---

[9] Wollaeger 137, 142.

[10] Brianus Waltonus, *Biblio Sacra Polyglotta* (London, 1657). In *Milton: Man and Thinker*, Denis Saurat claims that Milton knew Walton personally, and had the Polyglot bible at his disposal (252).

4. Brianus Waltonus, *Biblia Sacra Polyglotta* (1654-57). The Polyglot Bible's versions of Genesis propose a simultaneity of creations and a multiplicity of origins.

organized by typology but by discontinuity[11] (see illustration 4). Yet like the ledger book it resembles, Walton's version of the bible presupposes a balanced set of accounts. Moreover, while Luther had argued that scripture provides its own interpretation, the Polyglot bible puts this premise into operation. Interpretation could truly "begin all over again" when grammatical errors and false idioms were finally collected.[12] But the result was that now comprehensible in any language, biblical history no longer carried any weight. Taken out from behind the veil of sacred history, Reformation scriptures were exhibited like the tabernacle's secret contents and "recontextualized within a history of historical documents as fragments from a lost world[,] impinging on the present [like] so many museum pieces"[13] (see illustration 5).

Jason Rosenblatt argues that Milton's "recontextualizations" have different results, however, because they continue to sanction authority: "Milton sees himself as a moral archaeologist picking up shards of truth banned for years in custom and error."[14] Similar results were produced through the efforts of John Selden, whose antiquarian interests included extensive researches into Hebraic legal codes, culminating in the *Uxor Hebraica* (1646), a massive compendium of ancient nuptial rites and marriage customs. Like Milton's divorce tracts, this work is primarily occupied with the conditions under which a man could repudiate his wife.[15] So striking is the way these antiquarian pursuits appear intent on dislodging contemporary materials. There are other important connections between Milton's and Selden's work, though. Unlike the Polyglot bible, which confidently sidesteps—or straddles—these issues, Milton's and Selden's "moral archaeology" exposes Renaissance ambivalence about history by implicitly raising questions like: In what ways

---

[11] Focusing on Renaissance New Testament scholarship written in Latin, Debora K. Shuger does not examine polyglot bibles at length in *The Renaissance Bible: Scholarship, Sacrifice, and Subjectivity*, but she does briefly describe their columns of text as "stratified divisions" (23). Her broader description of the ways sacred narratives were bolstered by secular researches seems apt for this discussion, as well as her claim that "Renaissance biblical narratives exerted a synthetic, centripetal pull on a disparate range of discourses and disciplines . . . [consequently they need to be read] as *cultural* documents in the broadest sense" (5).

[12] See Gerald L. Bruns, *Hermeneutics Ancient and Modern* (140).

[13] Bruns 149.

[14] Jason Rosenblatt, *Torah and Law in Paradise Lost* (98).

[15] Rosenblatt claims that Milton and Selden had met by 1643 or 1644 (87). See also Eivion Owen, "Milton and Selden on Divorce."

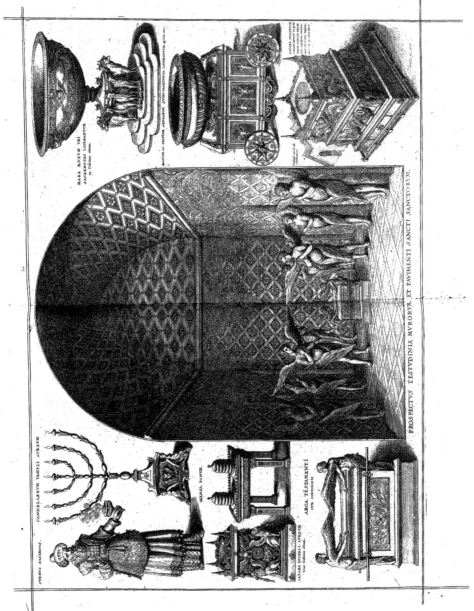

5. Brianus Waltonus, *Biblia Sacra Polyglotta* (1654-57). Once the ritual tools housed inside the sacred temple are

does the past antedate the present? How does the present point to the past? On what grounds can we compare the two? And what holds the two constructs, like the columns exhibited in Walton's Polyglot bible, together?[16]

***

We might return to our initial example, not for an answer but for a rationale. Perhaps Milton (unlike Othello) allows Eve to "go on" because the wife who abandoned him eventually returned. "Long choosing and beginning late," Milton's plans for a *Paradise Lost* are sidetracked when his marital bliss is shattered and his first wife Mary Powell, whom he married in June 1642, leaves him a few months later to return to her father's house. A year after her departure, a tract entitled *The Doctrine and Discipline of Divorce* (1643) appears, followed by a second edition a year later. In close succession appear three more tracts: *The Judgement of Martin Bucer* (1644), *Tetrachordon* (1645) and *Colasterion* (1645). Mary Powell then returns and the arguments for divorce subside.

Many readers have wrestled with this history to pinpoint strains in the divorce tracts between Milton's incipient feminism and chronic misogyny or between a newfangled egalitarianism and old-fashioned hierarchism.[17] Other readers have consulted it to untangle the closeknit threads of sacred ambitions and profane accidents in *Paradise Lost*.[18] James Grantham Turner, for instance, concludes that:

> The divorce issue, exploding with the Civil War, forced [Milton] to treat a personal episode as a national crisis, and it plunged him into a total engagement with the story of Genesis, which he was half inclined to dismiss as 'remote' or to convert into a Platonic myth. Without the divorce tracts, Milton might have produced a turgid Arthuriad or Cromwelliad instead of *Paradise Lost*.[19]

---

[16] A similar set of questions are posed by rabbinical scholars like Daniel Boyarin, who seek to redress Pauline claims about how the "spirit" of the Gospels replaces the "dead letter" of the Torah. Instead, Boyarin argues, a Christian confusion over the meaning of history is at work. See "The Subversion of the Jews: Moses's Veil and the Hermeneutics of Supersession."

[17] See Stephen Fallon, "The Metaphysics of Milton's divorce tracts" (87); and Mary Nyquist, "The genesis of gendered subjectivity in the divorce tracts and in *Paradise Lost*."

[18] See Annabel Patterson, "No Mere Amatorious Novel?"

[19] James Grantham Turner, "The Intelligible Flame" in *John Milton* (75). In

I would argue that the "divorce issue" forces Eve (rather than
Arthur) to become the idol Milton smashes. With this in mind, we
might explore Eve's literary function and obsolescence and retrace
her poetic rebirths and disappearances in terms of specifically historiographical pressures. The "divorce issue" provides Milton with
a potent metaphor and rich literary method. Etymologically meaning to turn away, the term "divorce" does not specify a direction or
signal a final goal (OED). For Milton, it serves at once as a means
to reclaim old positions and a method of revision, a way both to
review the past and reconstitute the present.

Created after the rest of Eden is finished, Eve is produced as supplement and obstacle, buried prize and secondhand fiction. Like
Mary Powell, Eve jointly functions as source and result, cause and
effect, since another contest being waged whenever Eve resurfaces
in the poem is between past and present. We see this when, even
after Eve arrives on the scene, Adam introduces her as a vision,
something he's dreamed of (8.460-77, 482). Moreover, when Eve
recounts her genealogy in book 4 (449-76), it is the story of her
being educated about her origins (482-86) so that she might "invis-
ibly [be] thus led" (476).[20]

Eve's abject status continually locates her in *Paradise Lost*, and
Milton's poem dutifully catalogs her displacements. Her birth is
really an awakening from sleep which "reposes" her (4.449-52), and
she continues to recede from view in the rest of *Paradise Lost* so that
her presence is never required in Paradise. In books 8 and 11, she
is absent from the angelic narrations. After eating the apple, Eve
worries that: "I shall be no more,/ And Adam wedded to another
Eve" (9.827-28). When Adam later relates his own birth narrative,
he recounts the creation of an unnamed helpmeet who then disappears. The first image we have of Eve from her husband is as a fugi-

---

Milton and the Idea of Matrimony: A Study of the Divorce Tracts and Paradise Lost, John
Halkett offers a similar reading, commenting that in the divorce tracts Milton
descends the Platonic ladder, since his depiction of unhappy marriages repeatedly
converts men into beasts (93). See also Sirluck's introduction to the divorce tracts
(*CPW* 2:137-58).

[20] Nyquist explores this issue in detail, explicitly raising the question: "Why does
Milton have Eve tell her story of her earliest experiences first, in Book 4? Why, if
Adam was formed first, does Adam tell *his* story to Raphael *last*, in Book 8?" (115).
She argues that the "narrative distribution" of their experiences is "ideologically
motivated," and claims that following the natural order would have made Eve
seem like a necessary supplement (115, 119). See also Stanley Fish, "Wanting a
Supplement: the question of interpretation in Milton's early prose."

tive, more a figure for the apocryphal Lilith[21] who shadows the perimeter of Eden than the "present object" Eve ultimately calls herself in book 10 (996).[22] Milton's treatment of Eve reflects Renaissance religious and political anxieties Shakespeare also explored about which texts were authoritative, or which conversations counted. But Eve's problematic status points to anxieties experienced at an even deeper level, over just which cultural memories ought to be repressed.

***

When they recovered Hebrew materials including Midrash, the Talmud and other rabbinical commentaries in order to shape a more authoritative scripture, many Protestants were forced to confront apocryphal texts. Some reformers simply claimed the Gospels were prior to the biblical canon and thus evaded the problem of the apocrypha entirely.[23] At least Luther is more openly ambivalent. "I so hate Esther and II Maccabees," he claims, "that I wish they did not exist. There is too much Judaism in them and not a little hea-

---

[21] In the kabbala, Lilith was Adam's first wife whom God introduced when Adam was seen coupling with animals. But Lilith quickly abandons Adam after they fight over lovemaking positions. Obliquely mentioned only once in the Torah (Is 34:14), Lilith is described by Harold Bloom as a "column left alone of a temple once complete." See *Figures of Capable Imagination* (265). According to kabbalistic legend, Lilith is a hag or succubus (etymologically, one who lies under) who nightly haunts paradise seducing the sons of men. The etymology also suggests a "screech owl" or "lamia" (Vulgate). Some rabbinical instructions record how she is exorcised with formal divorce imagery.

There are oblique references to Lilith in *Paradise Lost*, too. She might be one of the "millions" of creatures Adam describes to Eve who nightly walk the earth (4.677-78); Eve may also allude to Lilith in acknowledging her own limitations to her husband: "I chiefly who enjoy/ So far the happier Lot, enjoying thee/ Preeminent by so much odds, while thou/ Like consort to thyself canst nowhere find" (4.445-449). Milton would have recognized the Lilith figure who haunts Spenser's *Epithalamion* as the "shriech Oule" (l. 345) the bridegroom tries to ward off when the newly-married couple retires for the evening. See *The Yale Edition of the Shorter Poems of Edmund Spenser*. Connections between Spenser's *Epithalamion* and Keats' *Lamia* are explored by Elizabeth Mazzola in "Marrying Medusa." See also *The Analogy of the Faerie Queene*, where James Nohrnberg links Duessa to Lilith (228-39).

[22] The term "present object" is also applied to Hamlet's father's ghost (1.1.161). France calls the disowned Cordelia Lear's "best object" (1.1.213).

[23] See John Cosin, *A Scholastical History of the Canon of the Holy Scripture or the Certain and Indubitate Books thereof as they are Received in the Church of England* (London, 1657); and William Whitaker, *A Disputation on Holy Scripture, against the Papists, especially Bellarmine and Stapleton* (1588).

thenism."[24] Typically, the historical solution to this problem had
been to suppress apocryphal materials yet again. As Frank Kermode
explains, after the closing of the biblical canon in 100 C.E., those
books which had been hidden away for the wise now "acquired dys-
logistic overtones, and the apocryphal came to mean the false or
inauthentic."[25]

Miltonists like Wollaeger and Virginia R. Mollenkott have been
able to recover the influence of apocryphal texts on Milton's poetry.[26] In fact, Wollaeger maintains, "the neglected category of apocryphal texts operates as a third term between the poetic and the
sacred."[27] He goes on to argue that its liminal status is exploited by
Milton when the apocryphal Raphael, who was guarding the gate
of Hell during creation, asks Adam to recount his story in book 8.[28]
More recently, Rosenblatt has concluded that "the Hebraic factor
in the Edenic books does not annul Milton's radically Pauline theology, nor does Milton's Paulinism cancel his Hebraism. The
Hebrew Bible and the Pauline epistles are the principal matrices of
Milton's poetry."[29]

I think the presence of both traditions accounts for the discrepancies Turner detects in the divorce tracts. He argues that:

> The text of 'lost Paradise' is thus both 'vanisht' and ever-present.
> Moses's legislation, and Milton's heroic endeavors to restore it, rest
> on a central contradiction: they will lead us back to the Paradisal
> happiness by pushing to its logical conclusion the fact that it is
> beyond our strength ever to return there.[30]

---

[24] *The Cambridge History of the Bible. The West from the Reformation to the Present Day*
(6-7).

[25] Kermode 601.

[26] Mollenkott, "The Pervasive Influence of the Apocrypha in Milton's Thought
and Art"; and Wollaeger. Two of the most important early readings of Milton's
Hebraism were proposed by H.F. Fletcher in *Milton's Semitic Studies, and Some
Manifestations of them in His Poetry* and *Milton's Rabbinical Readings*. Fletcher has his
critics, however. That Milton's rabbinical Hebrew was quite poor is suggested by
Samuel S. Stollman, "Milton's Rabbinical Readings and Fletcher." For a broader
treatment of the relationship between midrashic materials and interpretive habits,
see *Midrash and Literature*.

[27] Wollaeger 151.

[28] Wollaeger notes that "In none of the four drafts of a projected tragedy [does]
the theme of *Paradise Lost* [refer] to Raphael. The first draft includes Michael; neither the second nor the third names any unfallen angel; and in the fourth it is
Gabriel who descends to the earth to describe paradise" (155 n 23).

[29] Rosenblatt 11.

[30] Turner (1993) 193-94.

Stephen Fallon has examined this "radical instability" on a stylistic level. He comments that "[r]hetorical practice mirrors theme in the divorce tracts. Dichotomies proliferate: body\soul, fault\blamelessness, necessity\freedom, grunting Barrow\gentle spirit, and so on"; "[w]riting about marriage and divorce," he adds, "Milton relies upon union and separation." But Fallon also notes that "[there is a] surplus of divorcive energy in Milton's endeavors to 'fadge together' in his tracts antipathetic arguments that, like individuals separated by 'natural anti-pathies,' refuse to be married."[31] While Fallon's conclusion is that Milton is basically addressing two different audiences (dualists, who need sex, and monists, who could do without), I would suggest that Milton is instead wrestling with two different but equally lively traditions in the Renaissance: Christianity and Judaism.[32]

The ongoing tension between patristic thinking and rabbinical argument in Milton's divorce tracts duplicates the frustrating conflicts he chronicles there between husband and wife. Taking up Mosaic law, which recognized incompatibility as a grounds for divorce, Milton argues:

> Thence this wise and pious Law of dismission now defended took beginning: He, therefore, who lacking of his due in the most native and humane end of marriage, thinks it better to part then to live sadly and injuriously to that cheerful covenant (for not to be belov'd & yet retain'd, is the greatest injury to a gentle spirit) he I say who therefore seeks to part, is one who highly honors the married life, and would not stain it: and the reasons which now move him to divorce, are equal to the best of those that could first warrant him to marry (*CPW* 2:253).

This text is troubled, however, by the sad history it recounts. Bitter reflections disturb its surface, and buried narratives unravel its forward-looking aims. The real question which poses itself, as Annabel Patterson acutely observes, is: "Who . . . is doing the divorcing, and

---

[31] Fallon 69-70.

[32] See Fallon 71. Joseph Wittreich makes a similar point, explaining that "*Paradise Lost* . . . emerges from a controversy over privilege and priority in interpretation (Genesis 1 versus Genesis 2, the Old versus the New Testament, the Hebrew versus the Christian Bible) and issues its own statement concerning that debate." See " 'Inspir'd with Contradiction': Mapping Gender Discourses in *Paradise Lost*" (135). According to Wittreich, the poem successfully accommodates "a variety of authoritative traditions (Hebrew and Christian) and different interpretive voices (patristic as well as rabbinical, Catholic as well as Protestant, humanist as well as Puritan)" (156).

at what moment does it occur?"[33] Just who is it "[w]ho is retained
but not to be beloved?" An analogous confusion about whether the
mistreated object is an unloved husband or unread text arises when
Milton describes his rescue of the long-neglected Mosaic scriptures
in his preface to the 1644 edition:

> Bringing in my hands an ancient and most necessary, most charita-
> ble and yet most injur'd, statute of Moses: not repealed even by him
> who only had the authority, but thrown aside with much inconsider-
> ate neglect under the rubbish of canonical ignorance; as once the
> whole law was by some such like conveyance in Joshiah's time (*CPW*
> 2:224).[34]

This contest over biblical sources and allegiances—and its solution,
as well—is recast in *Paradise Lost*, because the past is now separate
and frozen in Eve, a construct that if easily awakened is just as easily dismissed. As a result, we first meet Eve as a memory or, rather,
something already repressed.[35] Only after he had angrily dismissed
Desdemona does Othello maintain he can still recall his wife
(4.1.249). Yet Eve's birth narrative itself begins with her turning
away. After awakening, she reports:

> I thither went
> With unexperienc't thought, and laid me down
> On the green bank, to look into the clear
> Smooth Lake, that to me seem'd another Sky.
> As I bent down to look, just opposite,
> A Shape within the watr'y gleam appear'd
> Bending down to look on me, I started back,
> It started back, but pleas'd I soon return'd
> Pleas'd it returned as soon with answering looks
> Of sympathy and love (4.456-65).

Caught in a circuit of narcissism and myopia, her ambivalence ultimately finds more suitable lodging in Adam, whose first words upon
seeing his mate are "Return fair Eve" (4.481).[36]

---

[33] Patterson (1990) 93.

[34] There may be unintended irony here, for the "rubbish" to which Milton
alludes is the rubble of the Temple of Jerusalem, undergoing repair when the
Torah is discovered buried inside. See Bruns' account of the story (67).

[35] In a narrative designed to catalog firsts and outline providential history,
Milton must alter chronology in order to represent Eve: history has to be unwritten because Eve really has no place in it. See Nyquist's account of the tensions
between the two versions of Genesis.

[36] And after the fall, Adam chastises Eve: "Would thou hadst heark'n'd to my

The way Eve continues to slide in and out of narrative view seems to mirror Milton's ambivalence about his Hebrew sources. Perhaps, like the divorce tracts, these sources serve both as a point of departure and longed-for-goal in *Paradise Lost*. Or maybe the historical ideal is simply to be able to move back and forth between them. This is a precedent, of course, with which our first parents unsuccessfully experimented. With so many "looks [that] intervene and smiles," Eve wants to divide their labors in book 9, and proposes to Adam that they temporarily separate (214, 222).

***

> What does analysis uncover–if it isn't the fundamental, radical discordance of forms of conduct essential to man in relation to everything which he experiences?[37]

Of all the suppressed narratives and ruins collected in Milton's poem, the chronology of Eve is the most obscured and the most contested. She remains the most troublesome element in his apocryphal text, at once sacred afterthought, spurious hearsay, occult figure and floating signifier. If analyzing Milton's treatment of Eve is a way to gauge his complex relationship to apocryphal material, it also discloses his contradictory ambitions for *Paradise Lost* as sacred text. Joseph Wittreich, for instance, claims that: "Interpretive commonplaces are not explained, but explained away, by a poem that is itself (in the version we all read) a second edition and that in its last books portrays Eve as herself a second edition."[38] Surely, though, Milton's presentation of Eve indicates a troubled relationship to his own past as well, since the figure whose birth and absence are repeatedly recounted in *Paradise Lost* haunts the divorce tracts, too, in the specter of the wife repudiated in favor of a more paradisal marriage.

---

words, and stay'd/ With me, as I besought thee, what that strange/ Desire of wand'ring this unhappy Morn,/ I know now whence possess'd thee; we had then/ Remain'd still happy, not as now, despoil'd/ Of all our good, sham'd, naked, miserable" (9.1134-39). In other words, simply leaving Adam, as Olga Lucia Valbuena might argue, was a "divorsive act." See "Milton's 'Divorsive' Interpretation and the Gendered Reader" (118).

[37] Jacques Lacan, "The circuit," *The Seminar of Jacques Lacan. Book II* (85-86).

[38] Wittreich 155-56. I would argue that Eve is both revised and unwritten, because at times she is removed from a sacred context altogether.

The same Reformation debates surrounding apocrypha over how to establish their sacred standing or determine exactly what they illustrate encircle Eve. In both cases, the problem is repudiating something which might be, if only secondarily, one of God's creations. There are other questions we might ask, however. By what principle is Eve displaced and reclaimed again and again in the poem? What is being synthesized in Milton's dialectics of repudiation?[39] I think that drawing on apocryphal materials–which not only describe angels and devils, but offer additional reasons for divorce besides adultery[40]–provides Milton with a method for experimenting with the ontological categories of past and present, vision and reality, memory and actuality. This possibility is repeatedly introduced in *Paradise Lost*. For one thing, the bodies of Adam and Eve may eventually disappear if all goes well (book 5). Conversely, Raphael warns, Adam might sink to the status of a beast in stooping to worship Eve (8.579-82).

These possibilities were not restricted to Milton's Paradise. Closely allied with reformist imperatives, colonial agendas and archaeological impulses, Renaissance historiography becomes more and more adept at producing ruins. Church and state offices at this time are busily deposing a king, mutilating icons,[41] disposing of Arthur, and inventing divorce (tricks which, in *Othello*, still required a handkerchief). At the same time, early-modern travel lore and anthropology get more precise at delimiting the non-existent or non-essential. But the long-devalued and now-recovered apocrypha permit Milton a wider range of epic possibilities and casualties. They provide him with an endless stream of faulty originals and discarded alternatives, and thus furnish a bottomless site for the production of knowledge and history.

H.F. Fletcher suggests that Milton was probably familiar with Buxtorf's rabbinical commentary in which Lilith figures largely.[42]

---

[39] Valbuena supplies one answer, suggesting that for Milton divorce was a more potent political metaphor than marriage (118). Halkett likewise notes that divorce in *Paradise Lost* is a creative act (2). And Patterson (1990) suggests that, in *The Doctrine and Discipline of Divorce*, Milton "introduces the 'scanning of error' as a narrative principle" (89).

[40] See Mollenkott 29.

[41] Loewenstein describes iconoclasm as "an essential means of effecting historical change" (5).

[42] Some of the implications (and problems) of Fletcher's book-length argument in *Milton's Rabbinical Readings* are cited by Rosenblatt (84, 97). See also Charles Cutler Torrey, *Apocryphal Literature: A Brief Introduction*.

But some of these ontological possibilities had already been taken up before Eve was fashioned out of a rib: Hamlet finally assumes the place of a ghost, Spenser's Florimell is doubled by a snowman, the knight Guyon is really an elf, and Prince Arthur spends his youth hibernating in faeryland. The faery queen herself, who visits Arthur in a dream (1.9), evokes what the rabbis called the "night fairy" Lilith's seductions. And as Milton himself reminds us, Henry VIII's researches into divorce, annulment, ex-communication and papal fallibility comprise a similar set of forays into those "vail'd" regions.[43] In each of these cases, the past collides with the present because they are construed from an entirely different set of materials.

One could even argue that seventeenth-century history is organized by the endless stream of originals in the pool which so absorb Eve. They are doubled at this same time by the kabbalistic invention of the *golem*, an artificial anthropoid created by Jewish mystics to challenge Christian humanistic learning. This plot backfires, however, when the golem reveals their project to be bankrupt, arriving on the scene only to announce that "God is dead."[44] The fulfillment of kabbalistic history here coincides with sacred obsolescence. As I explored in the first chapter, another painful lesson in ontology was provided by the false prophet Sabbatai Sevi, whose pronouncements shook Palestine and all of Europe in 1665 when he announced that he was the Messiah, only to apostatize to Islam a year later.[45]

Herself a comparable piece of apocryphal history, Eve can likewise absorb doctrinal disturbances. But there are still other apocryphal analogies. R.W. Southern explains why Islam, whose "contradictions" had been intolerable to the medieval imagination, no longer represented a threat to early-modern Europe. Previously, Southern writes, Islam's ontology had not only challenged Christian doctrine but subverted itself, for

---

[43] Milton argues that no man "should . . . be forc't to retain in society to his own overthrow, nor to hear any judge therein above himself. It being also an unseemly affront to the sequester'd & vail'd modesty of that sex, to have her unpleasingnes and other concealements bandied up and down, and aggravated in open Court by those hir'd maisters of tongue-fence. Such uncomely exigences it befell no lesse a Majesty then Henry the 8th to be reduc't to . . . "(*CPW* 2:347).

[44] See Gross 50; Moshe Idel, *Golem: Jewish Magical and Mystical Traditions on the Artificial Anthropoid*; and Scholem (1971).

[45] This disaster is recounted by Scholem (1973). Also see Philip Beitchman's unpublished essay, "Milton and Cabala, Reconsidered."

what was to be made of a doctrine that denied the divinity of Christ
and the fact of his crucifixion, but acknowledged his virgin birth and
his special privilege as a prophet of God; that treated Old and New
Testaments as the word of God, but gave sole authority to a volume
which intermingled confusingly the teachings of both Testaments;
that accepted the philosophically respectable doctrine of future
rewards and punishments, but affronted philosophy by suggesting
that sexual enjoyment would form the chief delight of Paradise?[46]

In the "vastly extended world picture of the seventeenth and eighteenth centuries," Europe subsumes America and so conducts its
own history westward, rewriting the East in the process.[47] Like New
World exploits, *Paradise Lost* suggests how the establishment of traditional (be they national or theological) boundaries coincides with
their transgression.[48]

Conclusion

Perhaps Islam was no longer a threat because, like *Paradise Lost*, it
now could both expose and contain cultural images normally
repressed. More frequently, such dreams to abolish history collapse
into literature, which increasingly becomes a vehicle for experiences
we cannot have or possibilities we have deliberately excised. In
Civilization and its Discontents (1930), Freud describes such imaginative
collapse as sublimation. But less than a decade later, he proposes in
Moses and Monotheism (1939) to recover what is lost in the process.
He explores Moses in some of the same ways I have been reading
Eve, as false prophet, renounced choice, and finally buried alternative. Freud also theorizes how biblical narratives like Exodus actively push aside their founders:

> The distortion of a text is not unlike a murder. The difficulty lies not
> in the execution of the deed but in the doing away with the traces.
> One could wish to give the word 'distortion' the double meaning to
> which it has a right, although it is no longer used in this sense. It

---

[46] R. W. Southern, *Western Views of Islam in the Middle Ages* (6).
[47] Southern 12.
[48] See Jacqueline Kaye, "Islamic Imperialism and the Creation of Some Ideas
of 'Europe'" (66).

should mean not only 'to change the appearance of,' but also 'to wrench apart,' 'to put in another place.'[49]

Yosef Hayim Yerushalmi carries this analysis one step further, suggesting that, "as a historical essay, *Moses and Monotheism* offers a singular version of history as essentially a story of remembering and forgetting. To be sure, this is analogous to Freud's conception of the life history of the individual. What has been overlooked is how strangely analogous it is also to the biblical conception of history, where the continual oscillation of memory and forgetting is a major theme through all the narratives of historical events."[50]

Freud claims that the text of *Moses and Monotheism* was written twice over: he had tried to put it away "but it haunted [him] like an unlaid ghost."[51] Clearly, one of the reasons Freud wanted to bury the story was because the "unlaid ghost" of Moses puts a face on forgetting and simultaneously serves as a mnemonic device, like the golem, which dislodges Hebrew culture. In the same way, Milton's classical allusions in *Paradise Lost* repeatedly point to literary tradition as bankrupt.

It is a commonplace that history must wait for its subjects to be dead. Less commonly recognized is history's obsession with failures and its appetite for relics. Like Milton, Hebraists such as Luther and Selden were consumed by the divorce debate because–if, there, personal histories were temporarily caught in a narrative loop–such stories "turning back" on themselves could create their own "feedback."[52] We might see *Paradise Lost* as a vast holding ground for such extraneous cultural materials or Renaissance fallout uneasily accommodated by providential schemes. Wrestling with the pieces of an abandoned ontology, Milton can shape a figure like Eve, a construct that proves that culture is working, since through it the past is continually displaced.[53] Rather than serving as biblical supplement, literature now allows history to prevent catastrophic confusion about

---

[49] Freud, *Moses and Monotheism* (1939, 1967) (52).
[50] See *Freud's Moses: Judaism Terminable and Interminable* (34).
[51] Freud (1939) 131-32.
[52] See Lacan (1991) 88.
[53] The importance of conversation in Miltonic marriage is equalled by the emphasis Freudian analysis places on it. In *Sigmund Freud and the Jewish Mystical Tradition*, David Bakan writes that the psychoanalyst "must receive the training (orally) in the training analysis. As the modern practicing psychoanalyst is quick to tell anyone, psychoanalysis is not to be learned from books" (35-36).

its sources and narratives (like that which rocked Europe in the wake of Sabbatai's apostasy) precisely by shifting epistemological focus onto these clear-cut mistakes. Even Sabbatai's followers ultimately decide that the messiah must go unrecognized.[54]

"[T]he more abject the failure," Lacan explains, "the better the subject remembers it."[55] Milton's history in *Paradise Lost* fastens on Eve as hermeneutical catastrophe and in this way is able, repeatedly, to let her go. In contrast, Othello learns about anachronism too late, turning Turk at the end of the play after murdering Desdemona and tragically reinventing himself as a threat long-since forgotten about (5.2.253-57). Possibly learning from Othello's mistake, Milton's divorce tracts more successfully accommodate personal failure and rescue apocryphal meanings. Inside them are contained the ruins of an abandoned marriage, shortly recovered when his wife returns home, but finally sanctified more than twenty years later in *Paradise Lost*.

It is not only *Paradise Lost* which Milton retrieves, however. Cleanth Brooks observed that Milton's Eve "anticipate[s] Freud's observations on the comparative difficulty the female has in the transition to adult heterosexuality."[56] In *Moses and Monotheism* Freud slightly adjusted those observations, however. Describing the latency period, he comments that "man is derived from a species of animal that was sexually mature at five years, and [this theory] arouses the suspicion that the postponement, and the beginning twice over, of sexual life has much to do with the transition to humanity."[57] If history as a catalog of failures and relics eases this transition, perhaps Eve's interrupted genealogy–like Mary Powell's "sweet, reluctant, amorous delay"–provides Milton with a necessary, even "charitable" lag.

---

[54] Scholem (1971) 61. Bakan sees Sabbatai's revolutionary movement (and its repression) as paradigmatic for Freud (viii, 25, 132). Bakan also makes an interesting case for linking Freud's patient Dora–as a collection of hermeneutical possibilities and errors–with "Torah" (247). Patterson (1990) similarly links Milton's evasions with Freud's use of euphemism in describing his treatment of Dora (101 n18).

[55] Lacan (1991) 85-86.

[56] Quoted by Nyquist 122.

[57] Freud (1939) 94. Patterson (1990) makes a similar point: "If writing is, as some think, the art of *not* saying what one means, the most profound avoidance, some of Milton's finest writing occurs in the effort to conceal from his readers and probably from himself the precise effect on his psyche of the long-delayed induction into heterosexual experience" (98).

PART TWO

LOST CAUSES

CHAPTER FOUR

THE TRAGEDY OF MARIAM AND THE CORPSES OF KINGS

Introduction

Freud's *Totem and Taboo* suggested that the most natural form for religion to assume is the body of the patriarch. But in this chapter, I explore how the dimensions of patriarchal bodies became increasingly harder to discern during the Renaissance. The period's fascination with shaping and maintaining the outlines of female bodies has already been described by Peter Stallybrass;[1] yet there seems to be a similar, if more subtle, investment in the lineaments of male bodies, and a more intense anxiety behind their designs. Hal's eulogy for Falstaff, for instance, deflates the noble sentiments surrounding Hotspur's body, and Hamlet is clearly torn between his father's ghost and Yorick's skull as proper mnemonic devices. Another set of difficulties–ones I propose to examine here in terms of their metaphysical, historical, and religious dimensions–operates behind the ambivalent responses to the body of the dead king in Elizabeth Cary's *Tragedy of Mariam, the Fair Queen of Jewry*.

This ambivalence is very different from the nostalgia Shakespeare attaches to Antony's corpse. Yet both Shakespeare and Cary are deeply concerned with the problem of disentangling the historical imagination from patriarchal bodies. That Mariam's acceptance of Herod's death could resemble a moral evasion suggests just how powerfully even emptied cultural spaces continue to organize histories and stabilize pieties. Another example of the anxieties surrounding patriarchal bodies (what constitutes them, what dissolves them) is at work in Reformation polemic over transubstantiation, the Catholic doctrine which stipulated that Christ's body and blood were actually present at the eucharistic sacrifice of the mass. I argue that these debates over the shape and extent and number of patriarchal bodies inform the "crisis of historicity"

---

[1] Peter Stallybrass, "Patriarchal Territories: The Body Enclosed."

Mariam undergoes, confronted with a range of mnemonic devices and the competing versions of the past they signal or submerge. But these debates also point to a larger shift in the Renaissance moral imagination, one now haunted by holy ghosts and obsessed with sacred remains.

***

Elizabeth's presence on the throne, then, was not the only source of Renaissance confusion over the precise lineaments of patriarchal bodies, be they royal, theological, or more-pervasive domestic versions. In fact, such confusion could work the other way around, so that the conflated image of the biblical tyrant Herod grew more and more synthetic during this time. While his image was projected first onto Henry VIII because of Henry's singular marital woes,[2] Cranmer and even Elizabeth herself were eventually likened to Herod,[3] and similar associations later attached themselves to James' absolutism.[4] It is extraordinary how long-lived Herod's image actually was, especially because a "traditional part of his iconography" was "physical pain, distortion and decay."[5]

A more complex if more tractable set of metaphysical problems accompanied the heated Reformation polemic surrounding transubstantiation. The Fourth Lateran Council had established the terminology and dogma of transubstantiation in 1215 (although the neologism *transubstantio* had been introduced a century earlier).[6] At the same time, Peter Lombard tried to pin down the logical features of this theological decision, explaining that:

---

[2] See Ferguson and Weller's introduction to Elizabeth Cary, *The Tragedie of Mariam, The Fair Queen of Jewry* (153 n9). All subsequent references to Cary's text will be to this edition.

[3] William Allen, *A True, Sincere, and Modest Defense of English Catholics* (1584), quoted by Eamon Duffy in "William, Cardinal Allen, 1532-1594." Allen, a witness at Cranmer's Oxford trial, described the Archbishop as that "notorious perjured and oft relapsed apostate, recanting, swearing, and forswearing at every turn." Allen's *Memorials* also likens Elizabeth to Herod (Duffy 282).

[4] See Shuger (1990) 210-11.

[5] See Margaret W. Ferguson, "Running on With Almost Public Voice: The Case of 'E.C.'" (66 n48); and Rebecca Bushnell, *The Tragedies of Tyrants: Political Thought and Theater in the English Renaissance* (87).

[6] Additional background is supplied by Joseph Goering, "The Invention of Transubstantiation." (147).

In Christ the saving victim was offered once. Then what of ourselves? Do we not offer every day? Although we do offer daily, that is done for the recalling of his death, and the victim is one, not many. But how can that be—one and not many? Because Christ was immolated once. For this sacrifice what corresponds to that sacrifice of his: the same reality, remaining always the same, is offered and so this is the same sacrifice. Otherwise, would you say that because the sacrifice is offered in many places, therefore there are many Christs?[7]

Refuting the troubling hypothesis of many Christs, the solution Lombard offered was not, however, a durable one. Prompted by Protestant reform, the Council of Trent in 1562 elevated its position to a doctrine and formally reaffirmed that Christ was indeed present at the eucharistic sacrifice of the mass. Calvinists would continue to fault Catholic literalism; other reformers like Samuel Johnson applied Renaissance laws of physics to argue that Christ could not be in two places at once;[8] from early on, Lutherans had attacked the doctrine from a historiographical standpoint, claiming that Christ's sacrifice at the Last Supper was a unique event which could only be commemorated, not repeated.

These interpretive difficulties over the status of dead or missing bodies were not confined to religious tracts. Conflicting readings of Christ's statement *Hoc est corpus meum* (this is my body) are foregrounded in Spenser's *Faerie Queene*, where the faery queen's "real presence" is only detected by Prince Arthur in a dream (1.9). Similar confusions are located alongside the political problem of retrieving prisoners' bodies posed at the opening of *1 Henry IV*, and the continued absence of these bodies silently undermines Hal's own position as "heir apparent." That a royal patriarchal body be displayed is not only an urgent political requirement but a sacred need, I think, for Reformation culture. If Macbeth's head can

---

[7] *Petri Lombardi Libir IV Sententiarum*, lib IV, dist. 12, cap. 5. Quoted by Francis Clark, S.J., *Eucharistic Sacrifice and the Reformation* (75-76). See Clark's eighth chapter, "The English Reformers' Own Opinions and Teaching about the Eucharistic Sacrifice Seen in the Theological Context" (127-76); and Preserved Smith, *A Short History of Christian Theophagy*. Almost fifty years after the Fourth Lateran Council, the feast of Corpus Christi was established (see Smith 83). Also of interest are the Grail legends which begin to circulate at this time.

[8] Samuel Johnson, *The Absolute Impossibility of Transubstantiation Demonstrated* (London, 1688). Johnson's treatise supplies geometrical proofs (32) in addition to rare common sense: "Now if that Bone cannot be contained in such a Crumb of the Sacrament, much less can the whole Body" (27).

finally be affixed on a pole, Coriolanus absolutely refuses to expose himself to the mob in exchange for their grateful worship.

While both King Arthur's whereabouts and Elizabeth's lineage were national obsessions, the resulting frustrations and proffered solutions seem also to be at work in eucharistic debates. One Protestant tract is authored by a "Mirth Waferer" who calls Catholicism a "iugling philosophie."[9] Another reformer (with, perhaps, a preternatural sense of the fast-food industry) compares the host to a "Jack-in-the-box."[10] But this derogatory phrase–like "popish plasma" or the more polite "angels meat"[11]–also suggests a sacred impulse to have it both ways, to inhabit the center and margins of philosophy, to organize and disrupt epistemological boundaries and hermeneutic circles.

***

These same confusions over patriarchal whereabouts are at work in *The Tragedy of Mariam, the Fair Queen of Jewry*, published by the Catholic Elizabeth Cary (1585-1639) in 1613. *Mariam* relates the story of Herod, King of Judea and his second wife Mariam and the chaos which erupts in their royal household when rumors of his death circulate. Ultimately these rumors turn out to be greatly exaggerated when the high priest (or "Great sacrificer") arrives with the news of "pleasing accidents," that Herod is alive (3.1.31; 3.2.40). But the king's absence has prompted a flurry of activity on both a domestic and political scale. Herod's disappearance and eventual reappearance provide Cary's readers with the opportunity to track patriarchal whereabouts, allowing them to travel along a hermeneutic circle and perceive firsthand the kinds of meanings history makes possible.

Although a closet drama intended for an elite audience, Cary's *Mariam* is also a political commentary consumed with matters of contemporary debate. It supplies an interesting parallel to many of Shakespeare's history plays, concerned as they are with disturbances

---

[9] See John Lechmere, *The Relection of a Conference Touching the Reall Presence* (140-43).

[10] Clark describes a number of reformers' complaints, including the reference to the host as a "Jack-in-the box" (178).

[11] See William Guild, *Three Rare Monuments of Antiquitie* (48).

of political legitimacy and royal genealogy. There are still other intriguing links to Shakespeare. If Hamlet warns the mousetrap players about "out-Heroding Herod," Cary performs such a deed by denying Herod's historicity and giving it to someone else.

More specifically, *The Tragedie of Mariam* explores the political and personal predicament of a wife who cannot abolish memory when she learns the rumors of her husband's death. Rather than feel liberated by the news, she now experiences the weight of the past more powerfully: in death, Herod seems to take up even more imaginative space. Because of his cruelties (he has murdered both her grandfather and brother), Mariam is torn between grief and joy, but Herod's absence also gives her a chance to rewrite the history between them. Cary seeks to expose anachronism as a profoundly intimate affair, something experienced at almost an intuitive level. In the process, Cleopatra is dropped from the play, although she had figured rather sympathetically in Cary's original, Flavius Josephus's *Jewish Antiquities*. Following the Catholic Thomas Lodge's 1602 translation of Josephus, Cary sets these events in Palestine, twenty nine years before the birth of Christ. She reworks an apocryphal account of empire so as to shadow a world on the verge of ideological eclipse, poised for a sacred reversal.[12]

I have outlined some of the ways eucharistic theology had begun to crumble during the Renaissance, and I will argue that this issue particularly shapes many conflicts of the play. If I focus on this matter rather than point (once more) to the resemblances readers often note between Mariam's domestic travails and Cary's own marital troubles,[13] there are other relevant connections to Cary's biography I do not wish to omit; and in the final section of this chapter, I explore the implications of Cary's public conversion to Catholicism

---

[12] Thomas Lodge, trans. *The Famous and Memorable Workes of Josephus* (1602). Maurice J. Valency notes that "[t]he fortunes of Herod are not merely the private fortunes of a petty prince; they are bound up with the fortunes of civilization, with the destruction of the old and the dawn of a new era. The execution of Mariamne is no simple domestic crime, nor even the climax of a vendetta; it marks the end of the great Maccabean house, and foreshadows the ruin of a people." See *The Tragedies of Herod and Mariamne* (68). Valency also reads Herod's jealousy as political, since Antony is an immediate threat for Mariam's love; but in Cary's version Antony is already dead. According to Menahem Stern, the first-century Jewish historian Josephus had as his contemporary the author of the apocryphal Book of Jubilees. See "Josephus and the Roman Empire as Reflected in the Jewish War."

[13] See Betty Travitsky, "The *Feme Covert* in Elizabeth Cary's *Mariam*"; and Sandra K. Fischer, "Elizabeth Cary and Tyranny, Domestic and Religious."

almost twenty years after *Mariam* was written.[14] This is an important event, I think, because a decision to convert to Catholicism
rather than return to it after Edward or Elizabeth's death meant
choosing a religion drastically reorganized by Protestant reforms,
forced to understand its history in a radically altered scheme and to
contemplate the body of its Savior as a carnal–and literal–fact.[15]

***

Cary's play details the troubled relationship between Herod and
Mariam after he has been recalled to Rome following Caesar's
defeat of Antony. Cary compresses the events of many years into a
single day so as to emphasize Mariam's ambivalence, compounded
when it is further revealed that Herod had ordered her death if he
should be killed. The announcement of Herod's death has set in
motion an array of impromptu political and domestic alterations:
his sister Salome plans to divorce her second husband Constabarus,
who can now release the political prisoners he has secretly hidden
from Herod in a "living tomb" (2.2.117); meanwhile, Herod's first
wife Doris plots to reinstate her son Antipater as royal heir. All are
clearly attempts to relocate patriarchal bodies in "this reversed
state" (1.2.204); all (but Salome's) are fearful "Should Herod's body

---

[14] Although it was entered on the Stationers' Register in December 1612, critics tend to date the composition of *Mariam* between 1602 and 1605; the lower limit
coincides with the publication of Lodge's translation of Josephus, and the upper
limit is based upon a dedicatory epistle to Cary's sister-in-law before her marriage.
If this estimate is correct, *Mariam* was probably written during the first year or so
of Cary's marriage, before the birth of eleven living children. Margaret W.
Ferguson (1991) claims Cary secretly converted during her early marriage, but in
1626 she was pressured to publicly convert to Catholicism while her husband
served as Lord Deputy in Ireland, a politically dangerous decision and one catastrophic for what already appears to be a poor marriage (37).

[15] Throughout Edward's reign, Catholics were still the majority, but Foxe's *Acts
and Monuments* (1563) would provide a new scheme for reading Catholic history,
according to F.J. Levy, *Tudor Historical Thought* (98-99). Elizabeth's professed
indifference may have dampened impulses to convert to Catholicism outright; her
ex-communication in 1570 would have forced Catholicism underground.

Cf. Barbara Lewalski, who focuses on the particular impact of Catholicism
upon female bodies in "Resisting Tyrants: Elizabeth Cary's Tragedy and History."
Writing Women in Jacobean England. Lewalski seems to read Cary's conversion as a
form of rebellion against her mother and husband, and suggests that: "Roman
Catholicism may have offered ladies [at court] some self-validation through the
honors it accorded the Virgin and numerous female saints" (186).

leave the sepulchre/ And entertain the sever'd ghost again" (2.1.81-82). But the most important transformation described is Mariam's opportunity to revise the past in the absence of this organizing figure. She not only admits: "Oft I have wish'd his carcass dead to see," but further hopes "the news may firmly hold" (1.1.18, 52). As a result, she can no longer summon affection for her husband when Herod returns. Angrily charging her with adultery, Herod sentences Mariam to death.

Shakespeare, whose *Othello* unfolds along similar lines,[16] provides many occasions when patriarchy absents itself only for women to take over the reins. Lady Macbeth presides over the banquet when Macbeth sees Banquo's ghost, and Volumnia reminds her son Coriolanus: "Thy valiantness was mine, thou suck'st it from me" (3.2.129). A more useful comparison might be made, though, between Mariam's assumptions and Cleopatra's manipulations of Antony's public image, bolstered especially whenever he returns to Rome.[17] Even when the dying Antony is brought to Cleopatra's monument, she refuses to descend from it to kiss him, fearing, she claims, the "imperious show/ Of the full fortun'd Caesar." Instead, Shakespeare's stage directions tell us, Cleopatra's women "heave Antony aloft to her" (4.15).

Cleopatra seems acutely aware of the jealousies of empire as well as of the mechanics of history. But she also knows that her lover can still become a god, if only because she has come up with her own technology–in this case, a makeshift set of pulleys–for transcendence. Cleopatra forces Antony out of history so as to preserve his image and protect cultural memory; in death, and "[e]specially in Cleopatra's dream," Jonathan Dollimore writes,

> Antony becomes at last what he always wanted to be, larger than life. But in the valediction there is also invoked the commemorative statue, literally larger than life: his legs bestrid the ocean. Antony becomes statuesque in a way that recalls that the statue is a literal, material embodiment of a respect for its subject which is inseparable from the obsolescence of that subject.[18]

---

[16] Ferguson (1991) draws this analogy (39).

[17] Ferguson and Weller's introduction provides an extensive discussion of parallels (41-2).

[18] Jonathan Dollimore, "Shakespeare, Cultural Materialism, Feminism and Marxist Humanism" (487).

In her mourning, however, Mariam rejects such embodiments. Early on, she lamented how her murdered brother's "youth and beauty" "both in him did ill befit a tomb" (1.1.41-42). Later, Mariam's mother Alexandra supplies her daughter with historical reasons for forgetting Herod: "Was he not Esau's issue, heir of hell?/ Then what succession can he have but shame?/ Did not his ancestor his birth-right sell?" (1.2.100-102). According to Alexandra, the same sacred history which explains Herod denies his authority; the same texts which document his existence call it into question. Alexandra does not simply argue that Herod is illegitimate. Instead, she reasons that as "Base Edomite," "damn'd Esau's heir" or "toad disgrac'd," historically speaking, Herod does not exist (1.2.84, 89). Of course, Henry VIII had relied upon a similar set of historical arguments, proposing his marriage to Katherine of Aragon be annulled because it had not even taken place.

***

> *Hamlet's instructions to the players*: O, it offends me to the soul to hear a robustious periwig-pated fellow tear a passion to tatters, to very rags, to split the ears of the groundlings, who for the most part are capable of nothing but inexplicable dumb shows and noise. I would have such a fellow whipped for o'erdoing Termagant. It out Herods-Herod. Pray you avoid it (3.2.8-14).

Donald R. Kelley has suggested how Renaissance legal studies revolutionized the writing of history following the example of Jean Bodin's *Methodus ad Facilem* (1572). But this change only became possible when biblical authority had itself been dissected by philology and sacred grammar and, in England, scrutinized by Henry's jurists.[19] While there had been what we might call a historical tradition before the Renaissance, it was not until the sixteenth centu-

---

[19] See Shuger, *The Renaissance Bible: Scholarship, Sacrifice, and Subjectivity*; and Donald R. Kelley, *Foundations of Modern Historical Scholarship: Language, Law, and History in the French Renaissance* (9).

ry that history regarded itself as a discipline.[20] Medieval historians had employed techniques poets borrowed, shaping narratives as romances or epics by tracking protagonists' failures or defeats.[21] Such methods were finally overturned by the unprecedented labors of genealogists, theologians, heralds and antiquaries which followed the reformers' destruction of monastic libraries. The once "exemplary value of history" yielded then to a "demonstration of variety and mutability of collective practices over time."[22]

We might take the figure of Herod as a case in point. The medieval Corpus Christi plays fashioned a Herod who stood as a figure for historical claustrophobia;[23] as Rebecca Bushnell notes:

> Who the 'Herod' of the mysteries was meant to be historically is itself confused in the cycles. In medieval literature 'Herod' characteristically conflates the identities of three different biblical Herods: Herod the Great, who was guilty of the slaughter of the Innocents; Herod Antipas, his son, who judged Christ and ordered the death of John the Baptist; and Herod Agrippa, the grandson of Herod the Great.[24]

Yet by adapting many newly-developed historiographical techniques, Cary aims to displace (or to "out") Herod, and to make him somehow responsible for the theatrical collapse of history he stages over and over again. Hamlet urges the players not to push Herod's histrionics too far, not to dissolve action from motive. Hamlet may also have Herod's faulty example in mind because of the tyrant's inability to protect his lineage, or even because Herod's composite image simultaneously deprives him of identifying material. Since Cary tells us Herod prizes Mariam's beauty as well as her elite sta-

---

[20] See Arthur B. Ferguson, *Clio Unbound: Perceptions of the social and cultural past in Renaissance England.*

[21] See A. Ferguson (1979) 32-33; and Quint (1993).

[22] Lawrence Manley, *Convention 1500-1750* (222). See also F. Smith Fussner, *The Historical Revolution: English Historical Writing and Thought 1580-1640* (xiv-xviii).

[23] Citing Bushnell, M. Ferguson (1991) points to connections between Henry VIII and Herod (66 n48). Ferguson and Weller further argue that: "Among the reasons to see connections between the Corpus Christi pageants representing Herod and Cary's *Mariam* is the latter play's suggestion that when Mariam meets her death, she is herself a figurative Innocent" (23).

[24] Bushnell writes: "At the same time that Herod's stage presence unites these different biblical identities, his own characterization spreads to other biblical kings. In particular, in the Wakefield (Townley) plays, Herod's features, recognizable from other mystery plays, seem to have tainted Caesar Augustus (Octavian) and Pilate (who elsewhere remains more individual)" (84-86).

tus (1.2.149-50), Mariam's historiographical efforts, like Hamlet's, have political consequences. Indeed, we get a glimpse of this possibility when Alexandra reminds her daughter that Antony had originally sought Mariam, and further speculates that it was Mariam, not Cleopatra, who belonged in Antony's chariot (1.2.195-96).

Still, Mariam's ambivalence (as Hamlet's predicament also suggests), reflects anxieties about interpretive abilities rather than over political power. Even Herod's outbursts could be viewed in this way. As Rosemary Woolf notes, the rage of the English Herod "springs not from political fears that another king will take his throne or from an overbearing response to defiance but from the intense hatred of one who believes himself a god and now finds that the true God has come."[25] In both the Corpus Christi dramas and Cary's *Mariam*, Herod must learn to conceptualize genealogy as different from history—and perhaps grasp the resulting shift in women's standing and power, something which occurs as well when fictive lineages of Arthur and Brutus were consulted by English historians.[26] In fact, such a transformation is what Cleopatra exploits, busily seeking to make Antony a god. When patriarchal bodies do not assure history, they must be rescued from it.

If Shakespeare and Cary both grasp the anxieties involved in Renaissance historiography and the ambiguities surrounding the "real presence," they nevertheless outline two very different ways of reading patriarchal bodies. Unlike Hamlet, Mariam does not offer a rival to Herod's imperialist version but a reading of it: the history she authors is "not simply a branch of knowledge" but more importantly "a mode of thought."[27] For this reason, I would qualify Elaine Beilin's description of the "martyr" Mariam's "transcendence" and her resemblance to Christ.[28] Besides the problematic

---

[25] Rosemary Woolf (203) quoted by Bushnell (85 n16).

[26] See Phyllis Rackin, *Stages of History: Shakespeare's English Chronicles*; and M. Ferguson (1991) 42-43.

[27] See Kelley 3.

[28] Elaine Beilin points out a number of important links to Christ's passion in *Mariam*, most notably the suicide of the butler. See "Elizabeth Cary and *The Tragedie of Mariam*." M. Ferguson (1991) further fleshes out the analogy to Christ (55). Beilin's claims resist the idea that Cary's interests were specifically historiographical. "While she was concerned [like other Senecan dramatists] with the political and moral issues of governance in her drama," Beilin argues, "Cary chose at the end of the play to view politics and morality from a transcendent religious perspective, one more suited to her own knowledge and personality" (62). Other readers have attached Cary more fully to specific historical situations or ideologies. See,

anachronism such a reading relies upon (when Cary's play investigates a world deprived of Christian transcendence), Beilin's thesis puts a limit on Cary's historical imagination, and ignores the fact that Mariam is trying to think through her chronology, not rebel against it. That, too, is the difference between Mariam and Salome, who simply wants to divorce Constabarus so that her lover "Silleus may possess his room" (1.4.317-18).

Indeed, without the interpretive crisis Mariam undergoes, the past, like Herod, is really still part of the present: furtive, implacable and tricky, its arrivals are unwelcomed and unplanned. Cary's play actually provides instructions for us to concentrate on Herod's immanence alongside his symbolic value. It also directs us to consider how Herod's function in the mystery plays–first performed in conjunction with the liturgical drama of the Mass–differs from his present role in Senecan drama.[29] Corpus Christi cycles celebrated "in integrated sequence" the incarnation of Christ: in this way, William Lewis writes, "man played at history-making, and he played out history in a theatrical arena to which he might repair for one long day, but only one day of the year."[30] From this delimited historiographical opportunity to the apocalyptic premonitions of Senecan drama (the fear that history might end), Herod's comic function is transformed into a tyrannical solipsism (so that he can override history).[31] Cataclysmic change and historical upset, once carefully orchestrated by the mystery cycles, are now projected inward. Diagnosing Herod's case as "imperial pathology," Gordon Braden claims:

> The logic of imperial paranoia reconstitutes civil war as palace intrigue, as matter not of votes and armies but of nuance, gossip, implication . . . . [the tyrant] effectively invents the significance of political acts, recreating in private a system of meanings once publicly accountable.[32]

---

for instance, Dympna Callaghan, "Re-reading Elizabeth Cary's *The Tragedie of Mariam, Faire Queene of Jewry*."

[29] Ferguson and Weller's introduction includes a very useful discussion of Corpus Christi pageants and Senecan drama (22-26). An invaluable reading of Senecan drama is provided by Gordon Braden, *Renaissance Tragedy and the Senecan Tradition: Anger's Privilege* (14-15).

[30] William Lewis, "Playing with Fire and Brimstone: *Auctor Ludens, Diabolus Ludicrus*" (51).

[31] See Braden 5.

[32] Braden 14-15.

Calvin's revision of the edition of Seneca prepared by Erasmus (1515, 1529) revived English interest in Senecan drama,[33] and members of the Protestant Sidney circle with whom Cary was familiar translated or composed a number of Senecan plays about Antony and Cleopatra.[34] There were other associations for Cary. At the age of twelve, she had taken issue with Calvin's *Institutes*;[35] now, she could resume the debate in another form. This use of Seneca for religious debate was not restricted to Cary, however. If, early on, the Corpus Christi plays were identified with the performance of the mass, Renaissance Senecan drama might be seen as addressing the fallout from reformation debates over the eucharist. When the Corpus Christi plays were finally recalled by the Archbishop in 1572, "out-Heroding Herod" became a criminal offense.[36]

But the "Mariamne dramas," as Maurice Valency notes, also "illustrate the evolution of a dramatic tradition over a period which is no less than coextensive with the entire history of tragedy in modern times."[37] This is the case, I would argue, because the Mariamne dramas theatricalize the failures of representation and enact the methods by which information is dramatically withheld or rendered immaterial. *Lear* and *Othello* are other examples, but Cary's play deals with these issues head-on. If in *The Faerie Queene* Spenser repeatedly provides Arthur's sleeping form as a tentative solution to eucharistic questions, the metaphysical and historical anxieties that transubstantiation provokes and utilizes are at work behind Cary's play.

***

Debora K. Shuger (1990) suggests that Reformation polemic about transubstantiation should be seen as part of a larger cultural tension between "rational thinking" (which separates subject and object, and

---

[33] See Friedman 257.

[34] See Nancy Cotton Pearse, "Elizabeth Cary: Renaissance Playwright" (606); Nancy H. Guttierez, "Valuing *Mariam*"; Lewalski 191; and Marta Straznicky, "'Profane Stoical Paradoxes': *The Tragedy of Mariam* and Sidnean Closet Drama."

[35] See Lewalski 181.

[36] Duffy (1992) describes how the Corpus Christi dramas met with official disapproval in the 1560s: "The surviving manuscript of the Townley plays is bowdlerized in accordance with this command, passages on the seven sacraments, especially the real presence in the Eucharist, scratched out and marked 'correctyd and not playd'" (580). On July 30, 1572, all copies of the plays were recalled by the Archbishop (581).

[37] Valency vii.

grasps this difference through history, ontology and epistemology) and a "participatory consciousness" (which unites subject and object and so transcends those categories).[38] Catholic, Lutheran, and Anglican denominations, along with more radical Puritan or Zwinglian sects, used uncertainties surrounding transubstantiation to argue over scripture, ritual, sacrifice and sacramentalism. In turn, Reformation debates over transubstantiation (or purgatory or scripture, for that matter) implied stances toward ecclesiastical hierarchy and royal authority. Christ's body and the king's body would, from this point on, always be at odds. "In the aftermath of the Reformation," Shuger notes, "the problem of social locus of the sacred was not only a religious problem, a question of how God manifests Himself in the world, but a political one, a question of whether a particular institution is holy and therefore powerful."[39]

At the same time, the questions Catholics and Protestants alike asked themselves were probably less nuanced than Shuger's often delicate formulations suggest. Basically, I think they wondered: Do we have the ability to conjure up Christ? Is our relationship to the sacred direct or indirect? The problem was that each group unconsciously claimed a "participatory consciousness," because the Reformation created a culture in which all groups craved direct access, and where all groups could maintain it through scriptural evidence while denouncing the "false rumours" of others (see *Mariam* 2.4.417).

Relying on the same patristic sources, for instance, contending theological camps found themselves awkwardly negotiating radically different conceptions of the past.[40] Much like any other piece of evidence debated by Renaissance historians, biblical models were increasingly evaluated according to which version was older or truer, which record offered a more "exemplary model" or provided a more "objective account." Such debates conflict with what Hans-Georg Gadamer calls an "effective-historical consciousness" "that understands the temporal distance separating present from past [and recognizes] that both past and present belong to the same continuum of historical tradition."[41] Rumors of Herod's death

---

[38] Shuger (1990) 19-20.
[39] Shuger (1990) 125.
[40] Shuger (1990) 6 n18.
[41] See Quint (1982) 49.

would therefore set in motion a "crisis of historicity," an overturn-
ing of political chronologies and power structures as well as an
inability to decide from what perspective to interpret events or even
where to situate oneself.[42] This crisis occurs when "[h]istory can no
longer claim to subsume all processes of change."[43] What Cary
makes clear, however, is that this crisis never requires or tolerates
the abandonment of history altogether. As Paul Gilroy more recently argues, historical dislocations can "ironically serve a mnemonic
function, directing us back to 'nodal' points in common history and
social memory."[44]

For this reason, Cary's intense interest in history does not finally
repudiate patriarchy, although it is less clear that her attitude should
be characterized as reactionary, as some critics have proposed.[45] If
Salome's rash decision to overturn Mosaic law and divorce
Constabarus is rejected in the play (4.8.1861-64), her grasp of biblical law nonetheless supplies Mariam with a hermeneutic example,
and reflects the wide-ranging creative impulses of Renaissance
jurisprudence. More important, *Mariam* chronicles a growing awareness of the past as something remote, differentiated from the self, at
odds at times with memory or reason. Cary also undertakes to
explore the tragic consequences of this awareness when Mariam
refuses the comforts of nostalgia and resolves to hate the husband
she's lost. Describing the dangers and attractions of nostalgia,
Walter Benjamin seems to repeat the outlines of Cary's play:

> To articulate the past historically does not mean to recognize it "the
> way it really was." It means to seize hold of a memory as it flashes
> up in a moment of danger . . . . In every era the attempt must be
> made anew to wrest tradition away from a conformism that is about
> to overpower it. The Messiah comes not only as the redeemer, he
> comes as the subduer of the Antichrist. Only that historian will have
> the gift of fanning the spark of hope in the past who is firmly con-
> vinced that even the dead will not be safe from the enemy if he
> wins.[46]

***

---

[42] Fredric Jameson, quoted by Bennington and Young, "Introduction: Posing
the Question." *Post-Structuralism and the question of history* (7).

[43] See Robert Young, *White Mythologies: Writing History and the West* (5).

[44] Paul Gilroy, *The Black Atlantic: Modernity and Double-Consciousness* (198).

[45] See Donald W. Foster's discussion in "Resurrecting the Author: Elizabeth
Tanfield Cary."

[46] Quoted by Gilroy 187.

> *Valeria to Virgilia*: "You would be another
> Penelope; Yet they say, all the yarn she
> spun in Ulysses' absence did but fill Ithaca
> full of moths" (*Coriolanus* 1.3.82-84).[47]

By believing the rumors that her husband is dead, Mariam insists
that patriarchs have bodies, too; in this way, she returns patriarchal
history to its rightful owner. Josephus's account in *Jewish Antiquities*
had focused on Herod's sister's Salome's unprecedented plan to
divorce her husband. But, in Cary's treatment, Mariam perceives a
historical window of opportunity and accomplishes this same feat
metaphorically, in her husband's absence actively wishing him dead.
Many Renaissance texts make this same qualified admission about
patriarchal bodies. Spenser and Milton both use and evade
Arthurian legend; and Shakespeare's roman plays recuperate and
bury fallen heroes. By 1688, Luther's own form would come to
serve as unstable surface on which to project eucharistic confusions:

> The *Devil* urges the nullity of *Luther's* Orders, upon the account of his
> being a *Sacrificing Priest*. The *Vindicator* (Luther's defender) distinguish-
> es upon him, That tho the Form (of making him a *Sacrificing Priest*)
> should be a little defective, yet where the Church intends to convey
> Orders, there they are actually convey'd; and his being made a
> Sacrificing Priest did not prejudice *Luther's* Orders at all. That is to
> say, he might be a *Sacrificing Priest*, and *a not-Sacrificing Priest*, by the
> same Form.[48]

It is because of such qualified admissions that relatively sophisticated antiquarian interests flourished alongside a massive production
of Renaissance ruins.[49] Historiography, an element of transubstan-

---

[47] Peggy Kamuf describes such an "interval" as "not simply some unrecorded
moment in the history of power but . . . a hiatus where power has momentarily
broken off its discourse." Exploring Virginia Woolf's revision of history in *A Room
of One's Own*, Kamuf asks: "Is [Woolf's text] an image, a metaphor with which to
call up the immaterial, the timeless and the imaginary defeat of power or is it
rather that which supports the metaphor, the denotative foundation on the basis
of which figurative space is constructed? A place in history which exists therefore
in social, political and economic contexts? Or a place which transcends these limits?" (8). See "Penelope at Work: Interruptions in *A Room of One's Own*."

[48] Thomas Deane, *The Religion of Martin Luther Neither Catholick nor Protestant, Prov'd
from his own Works* (1688) 20.

[49] See Joseph M. Levine, *Humanism and History: Origins of Modern English
Historiography*. Levine explains that Henry's dissolution of the monasteries also emptied out monastic libraries and scattered their holdings; but under the king's tute-

tiation rhetoric which eventually assumed a life of its own, found
itself plagued by uncertainty over what properly belonged to the
past and bewildered by "the vital questions of what is viable and
what is not."[50] Remembering also has a history it is eager to forget.
As Thomas Greene suggests, Petrarch's perception of historical distance had now come to serve, with mixed results, as a kind of epistemological bridge between past and present–something that, like
the eucharistic "jack-in-the-box," might easily come into play, or
remain surprisingly inert:

> New etiological myths had to be produced which could contain the
> facts of loss and anachronism, myths which could no longer assert the
> universal unity for which Dante wrote and fought. The Renaissance
> did produce such a myth or cluster of myths in its pervasive imagery
> of resurrection and rebirth, imagery still reflected in our period term
> . . . . [But] the characteristic risk of Renaissance imitation lay in the
> potential paralysis of its pieties, in a rhetoric so respectful of its sub-
> texts that no vital emergence from the tradition could occur. The
> diachronic itinerary circles back to its starting point or peters out in
> a creative desert.[51]

Cary avoids this problem because *Mariam* focuses not on etiological
myths but on eschatological ones. Her play, that is, uncovers not
only where history is grounded but what myths shape its ends,
which stories make visible its limits. In this way, Mariam's history
provides a dry run for Christian transcendence. But Herod learns
this lesson too late. He attempts to retract his command for
Mariam's death, only to discover that his wife has already been exe-
cuted:

> *Herod*: But art thou sure there doth no life remain?
> Is't possible my Mariam should be dead?
> Is there no trick to make her breathe again?
> *Nuntio*: Her body is divided from her head.
> *Herod*: Why, yet methinks there might be found by art
> Strange ways of cure; 'tis true rare things are done
> By an inventive head, and willing heart (5.1.87-93).

---

lage many old manuscripts were collected, and by 1546 an inventory of Roman,
Celtic and Saxon ruins was underway. Under Elizabeth, Archbishop Parker
formed a coterie of antiquaries to retrieve Anglo-Saxon remains and thereby
defend the Anglican settlement.
    [50] Gilroy 198.
    [51] Thomas Greene, *The Light in Troy: Imitation and Discovery in Renaissance Poetry*
(30, 39).

Conclusion

> The English Catholic community has bred
> some great historians, but they have not
> contributed much to its own history. Their
> reluctance is understandable, but a pity;
> for it has left the community uneasily
> related to its past, uncertain where to look
> for it and what to make of it, embarrassed
> or over-devout.[52]

Daniel Boyarin has commented that much of the cultural politics of "the West," "that is, the relation of 'Judaism' to
'Christianity,'" is really "a question of literary theory."[53] Cary's play
seems to steer clear of such mystifying questions; outlining Salome's
exchange of Palestine for Rome (1.5.362), she instead imagines the
pre-history of the West. Yet the religion Cary publicly converts to
in 1626, a post-Reformation Catholicism, might also be explored in
terms of literary theory or even examined as a cultural poetics with
less and less direct applicability to culture. Forced underground during Edward's brief reign and immediately resurrected when Mary
assumes the throne in 1553, Catholicism never again becomes part
of orthodox culture, despite–or because of–Elizabeth's indifference.
An abbreviated version of these theological collisions (and road-
blocks) was evident during the whole of Henry's reign. The king
first clashes with Luther and is awarded as Rome's "Defender;" but
he then breaks with Rome, dissolves the monasteries and repudiates
purgatory. After his death, English catholics make use of secret
chapels, hidden vestments, mutilated icons, and reconditioned altar
tables, so that relatively few sacred relics remained entirely unem-
ployed or obsolete. A critical problem for Reformation culture (and
one that New Historicists tend to ignore) was recovering representations which were not quite lost but repressed or temporarily hidden, images or symbols which underwent transformation but not
transubstantiation.[54] This helps us to observe that, like the "history

---

[52] John Bossy, *The English Catholic Community 1570-1850* (1).
[53] Daniel Boyarin, "The Subversion of the Jews: Moses's Veil and the
Hermeneutics of Supersession" (16).
[54] Shuger (1990) similarly comments that the difficulty with the New Historicist
division of beliefs into the orthodox and the subversive is that "so-called subversive ideas keep surfacing, however contained, within the confines of orthodoxy" (1).

of the West," the relation of Christianity to Judaism, or of Christianity to itself, is always unstable.

Another example of a barely recognizable sacred sign used to meet an almost identical sacred need was employed in the test of orthodoxy under Elizabeth, which involved taking communion in established Protestant churches. The rejection of transubstantiation had been the most hated of reforms under Cranmer during Edward's short reign, the last time there had been a Catholic majority in England. Cranmer rejected the doctrine of the "real presence," argued against the efficacy of the sacrament, and denied the mass was a sacrifice. After Cranmer, "eternity," as Malcolm Mackenzie Ross puts it, was no longer allowed to "puncture time."[55] Protestant communion was hardly then a concession to English catholics, since Elizabeth's test denied a history of eucharistic sacrifice even while maintaining the uniqueness of Christ's offering as historical event. Interestingly, though, Protestant communion could be "vicarious," one man taking the bread and wine for another. The physical act of consuming the host was still required, even if the carnality of the sacrifice had been overturned.[56]

We might align the repudiated doctrine of transubstantiation with the Catholic humanism at work in More's *Utopia*, displaced, as Jeffrey Knapp argues, "nowhere,"[57] or in terms of a Renaissance historiography which could successfully negotiate between past and present because, at the moment, it really belonged to neither. Like More, Cary had long practiced such metaphysical techniques and, from an early age, had tested their limits. One daughter recounts that as a child Cary helped prove the innocence of a woman accused of witchcraft. The woman had already confessed to a num-

---

A recent article in *The New York Times* indicates this problem persists even today. In "Lutherans Considering Sweeping Change," Gustav Neibuhr reports on a new and "sweeping proposal for closer ties" with allied Protestant churches. The plan (formally debated in Philadelphia, the site of another constitutional congress) would not merge churches but 'establish full communion' between Lutherans and other Protestant churches, allowing, for instance, for "exchanges of clergy members." Such a move would seem to increase the "real presence" of spiritual leaders and, in this way, perhaps acknowledge the eucharistic principles still retained by Lutherans.

[55] See *Poetry and Dogma: The Transfiguration of Eucharistic Symbols in Seventeenth Century English Poetry*.

[56] See Jean Delumeau, *Catholicism between Luther and Voltaire: a new view of the Counter-Reformation* (209). Delumeau's work is cited by Shuger (1990).

[57] Jeffrey Knapp, *An Empire Nowhere*.

ber of crimes, but Cary inquired whether she was also responsible for the death of Cary's uncle, standing nearby and listening to the proceedings. The accused fearfully admitted to this charge as well; but when questioned further acknowledged that she had been intimidated into confessing and so was exonerated.[58] This was not the only time Cary explored the tractability of patriarchal bodies, and towards the end of her life, she planned to smuggle her younger sons abroad to seminaries.[59]

The ease with which male bodies might disappear and gloriously reappear certainly encouraged Cary's labors. But such disruptions of epistemological systems and sacred narratives were, by and large, more troubling to the patriarchal bodies who remained. Probably at the same time she had begun drafting *Mariam*, Cary read a conservative defense of the Anglican settlement, Richard Hooker's *Laws of Ecclesiastical Polity* (1593), which took the position that transubstantiation occurs in the believer's heart, not at Mass.[60] Merely (if neatly) relocating the problem, Hooker's formulation removes sacred experience from history. Yet Hooker's contemporary, the Catholic Cardinal William Allen, worried that in saving history sacred experience would be emptied out. He lamented that many priests "said mass secretly and celebrated the heretical offices and supper in public, thus becoming partakers often on the same day (O horrible impiety) of the chalice of the Lord and the chalice of the devils."[61] According to Hooker's account, transubstantiation took place in reality "nowhere." But Allen feared the opposite was true: he was terrified that transubstantiation might take place everywhere.

---

[58] Recounted by Pearse 601-02.

[59] See Fischer 231. Interestingly, a recent, irate letter to the editors of *The New York Times* relies on a somewhat similar equation, inversely relating women's capacities to the real presence of Christ. Rejecting Father Richard O'Brien's "astonishing assertion" that "[t]here are literally millions of Catholics in the U.S. alone who see no reason why women can't be ordained," (Rev.) Allan Hawkins responds: "Maybe so. But recent surveys have also concluded that large numbers of Roman Catholics 'in the U.S. alone' do not believe in the Real Presence of Christ in the Eucharist—a belief indisputably central to Catholic life, faith and practice. That being so, it is hard to understand why Father O'Brien thinks it is so important that the Pope and the Vatican should be in step with contemporary American opinion."

[60] Lewalski treats Cary's rejection of Hooker's *Ecclesastical Polity* (183); see also Ferguson and Weller (4-5); and Shuger (1990) 40.

[61] Duffy (1995) 270.

CHAPTER FIVE

DEFYING AUGURY: PROTESTANT MAGIC IN *HAMLET*

Introduction

There is a lack of focus or epistemological wobble that complicates Hamlet's reasoning, severing physics from metaphysics, splitting theology from law, divorcing rhetoric from history, making it hard for him to decipher the past from the present. "[F]retted with golden fire," the "majestical roof" of the sky "appeareth nothing" to him "but a foul and pestilent congregation of vapours" (2.2.301-03). More serious, the Prince cannot draw conclusions or wrestle meanings from his ideas. Hamlet claims to feign "an antic disposition" (1.5.180). But he is unable to think chronologically, to establish precedents and read history as an ordered set of motives or solutions, or to see his father's death as something inevitable, natural, and finally, part of the past.

Hamlet's thinking only multiplies his confusions, and his insights often throw him off course. Every object he muses over becomes a black hole or lost cause, unhinged from and unsupported by the "sterile promontory" surrounding him. Timothy Reiss argues that Shakespeare's play is motivated by action and distraction, organized around moments when the burden of memory is overwhelmingly charged, or simply overwhelming.[1] But I suggest in this chapter that the events and meanings of *Hamlet* are interrupted more systematically than Reiss implies. Indeed, the play begins with the transfer of the burden of memory, opening at midnight when the king's sentries trade places. More clearly in the play the Prince stages at Elsinore, one representation immediately gives way to another, according to a logic which is not discursive or ritualistic (since it cannot be shared or repeated) but magical and dissociative.

Raphael Falco might have us view these dissimulative, dissolved representations as "instant artifacts," objects recovered by the

---

[1] Timothy Reiss, *Tragedy and Truth: Studies in the Development of a Renaissance and Neoclassical Discourse* (173).

Renaissance imagination only to be buried in the process of recovering other ones.[2] We are shown two more artifacts when the Prince lectures Gertrude about his father's unrivalled standing.[3] Instead of reifying the dead king's image, Hamlet produces two images, placing the god-like, unearthly king and father alongside its "counterfeit presentment" (3.4.54), the bestial, but all-too-human Claudius:

> See what a grace was seated on this brow,
> Hyperion's curls, the front of Jove himself,
>   . . .
> This was your husband. Look you now what follows.
> Here is your husband, like a mildew'd ear
> Blasting his wholesome brother (3.4.55-56).

The brothers are utterly dissimilar; like royal apples and oranges, there is no resemblance or connection between them.[4] What can be deduced from such failed analogies or mixed metaphors? What can be concluded, except the breakdown of epistemological systems which once held reason together?

Repeatedly in *Hamlet*, one semiotic system yields two different realities. The old ways of knowing the world are applied to a now-sharply different terrain, so that Hamlet might imagine the erotic appeal of his dead father. Such semiotic discrepancies only accumulate: Laertes' hasty revenge is crudely pitted against Hamlet's indecision; and Fortinbras' dynastic claims subsume the Prince's faulty memory.[5] Yet the play's capacity to sustain—and be informed by—two conflicting images characterizes Renaissance culture more

---

[2] I borrow the term from Falco, *Conceived Presences: Literary Genealogy in Renaissance England*.

[3] See Lupton's description of how Caravaggio's Baroque style 'performs a series of operations on its Renaissance original' (xvii). Displacing the eschatological narrative of a Catholic saint, Lupton argues that its Christian subject matter becomes classical.

[4] Marjorie Garber also focuses on this episode, to point out how "[r]epetition and the repetition compulsion are figured throughout *Hamlet*. But with a difference." Along with the anamorphic skull Garber describes—the shadow of mortality which disrupts Holbein's famous portrait of *The Ambassadors*—we might include these two images, alongside the image of the ghost of Hamlet's father. See *"Hamlet*: Giving up the Ghost." *Hamlet*. ed. Susanne L. Wofford (298).

[5] Greene (1991) describes the "changing status" of Renaissance signs employed in ceremonial and ritual performances, a change which ultimately enables Fortinbras to assume sovereign power at the end of the play. Greene proposes to articulate a missing sub-discipline which he terms "historical semiotics" (196); in part, this chapter proposes to trace the history of its absence.

widely.[6] Luther's plans to restore the church split it into two; and iconoclasm's loathing of sacred images imagines their power more forcefully. We might also include the way Queen Elizabeth completely inhabits the magical space once occupied by the Virgin Mary so as to prohibit transference and block metaphor.[7] A revised set of imaginative practices have taken shape, interpreting experience through a new lens or *ratio*, splitting the past into two and renting memory from knowledge. Hamlet's *Mousetrap* enacts the split graphically, so that the lack of focus becomes clear just at the moment when it should disappear, and any knowledge his play produces is trapped rather than exposed. Renaissance mimesis might be construed as a particularly forceful epistemological technique for making knowledge unnecessary.

***

John Dover Wilson analyzed the play scene extensively in *What Happens in "Hamlet"*, taking up questions like: Why is *The Murder of Gonzago* (the play Hamlet refashions) part of the players' repertory in the first place? Exactly where are the lines the Prince inserts? And why is Hamlet's play preceded by a dumb show?[8] It is the last of these questions that I will concentrate on over the next few pages, because the addition of the dumb show only heightens the semiotic disturbance outlined above:

> The trumpets sound. A dumb-show follows.
> Enter a KING and a QUEEN, the Queen embracing him and he her. She kneels, and makes show of protestation unto him. He takes her up, and declines his head upon her neck. He lies him down upon

---

[6] Mark Matheson similarly notes that while "[r]eligious discourse is integral to *Hamlet*," "Shakespeare's representation of religion is oblique and inconsistent . . . ." See "*Hamlet* and 'A Matter Tender and Dangerous'" (383). This theological inconsistency could be likened to Falstaff's story of multiplying men in buckram suits, for which Hal rebukes him: "These lies are like their father that begets them;/gross as a mountain, open, palpable" (2.4.220-21). See also Shuger, " 'Nor th' exterior nor the inward man resembles what it was': *Hamlet* and Christianity." Shuger claims that "in any given passage [in the play]–sometimes within a line–the ideological gears shift; the language of belief is suspended, infiltrated by quite different discourses." Shuger cites, as an example, the ghost from purgatory who uses Senecan discourse.

[7] See Roy Strong, *The Cult of Elizabeth: Elizabethan Portraiture and Pageantry*.

[8] John Dover Wilson, *What Happens in "Hamlet"*.

a bank of flowers. She, seeing him asleep, leaves him. Anon comes in another Man, takes off his crown, kisses it, pours poison in the sleeper's ears, and leaves him. The QUEEN returns, finds the King dead, makes passionate action. The Poisoner with some Three or Four comes in again. They seem to condole with her. The dead body is carried away. The Poisoner woos the Queen with gifts. She seems harsh awhile, but in the end accepts his love. Exeunt.

Critics are divided as to whether the dumb show simply duplicates the action of *The Murder of Gonzago,* and whether Hamlet was dismayed to see it performed after faulting "inexplicable dumb shows" in his earlier advice to the players (3.2.12).[9] Readers like W. W. Lawrence and Dieter Mehl point out, however, that the dumb show had continued to be a popular feature of the Elizabethan theatrical tradition.[10] Part of its appeal was probably related to the parallel theatrical experience offered by the mass. Dumb shows strenuously labor to produce a "visible word," as Augustine's terminology for the "real presence" had prescribed.[11] Mehl connects dumb shows to medieval *Corpus Christi* pageants because the representation of a murder was usually their subject. Similarly, O.B. Hardison notes that the elevation of the eucharistic host during the Latin mass (*repraesantatio Christi*) was a silent display which proved the alleged sacrifice.[12] Just as we see in Hamlet's play at Elsinore, dumb shows

---

[9] See W. W. Greg, "Hamlet's Hallucination." Greg argues about the sheer redundancy of the dumb show, asserting: "If the king could sit unmoved through the representation in pantomime of these events there is no imaginable reason why they should move him when acted with words. For the language of the play adds nothing to the pointedness of the allusion" (398). According to Greg, however, mimesis controls reality; influenced subconsciously by his knowledge of *The Murder of Gonzago,* what Hamlet had previously seen enacted later inspires the vision of his father's ghost. Greg himself has inspired almost a century of critics, although Stanley Cavell maintains that "no one has satisfactorily answered Greg's claim." See Cavell, "Hamlet's Burden of Proof." *Disowning Knowledge in Six Plays of Shakespeare* (180).

[10] W.W. Lawrence, "The Play Scene in *Hamlet*" (8); Dieter Mehl, *The Elizabethan Dumb Show: The History of a Dramatic Convention* (7, 24).

[11] Jaroslav Pelikan, *Reformation of Church and Dogma (1300-1700). The Christian Tradition: A History of the Development of Doctrine. Vol. 4* (190).

[12] O.B. Hardison, Jr. *Christian Rite and Christian Drama in the Middle Ages: Essays in the Origin and Early History of Modern Drama* (ix, 288). The connections between the dumb show and the mass may run even deeper: Garber offers a qualification of Mehl's claim, proposing to view the "transference" in a dumb show as an "artificial illness" (320-21). Just as in the eucharistic feast, the subject of a dumb show is never permanently disabled.

appear intent on transforming corporeal images into signs, convert-
ing the body into a locus of loss or site of "real absence."[13]

Intended or not, Hamlet's dumb show also suggests some of the
added burdens on theatrical representation—namely, to show more,
and mean less—when the eucharistic bread and wine were read by
Protestants as props or mnemonic devices rather than as Christ's
actual body and blood.[14] Enacting the same shift dumb shows carried out from purely ritual to increasingly representational modes,
the mass was no longer seen as magical sacrifice but as pedagogi-
cal tool.[15] This modification is reflected by a Renaissance theater
increasingly structured by conflicting theories of mimesis. "The real
change brought about by the Renaissance," Arnold Hauser maintains, "is that metaphysical symbolism loses its strength and the
artist's aim is limited more and more definitely and consciously to
the representation of the empirical world."[16]

Metaphysical symbolism had begun to lose its strength as early
as the thirteenth century, however. Jaroslav Pelikan argues that
from that time on, all great thinkers had tried to elucidate eucharistic dogma. Yet not until the Reformation was the evidence itself

---

[13] Horton Davies notes that "Zwinglianism was criticized as the doctrine of the
'Real Absence.'" *Worship and Theology in England: From Cranmer to Baxter and Fox,
1534-1690* (82). Still, Luther's position remained problematic as well. Raymond
Waddington comments that Luther's radical eucharistic doctrine, "more than any
other aspect of his theology[,] frustrated the acceptance of Lutheranism in
England." See "Lutheran *Hamlet.*" (28-9).

[14] The Diet of Worms, a German council convened in 1521 to challenge
Luther's teachings, is recalled by Shakespeare when Hamlet describes Polonius's
body as "food for worms" (4.3.19-28). See the Arden edition 340 n21;
Waddington; and Matheson 391.

[15] Hardison ix; 288. Cf. Robert Weimann, *Shakespeare and the Popular Tradition in
the Theater: Studies in the Social Dimension of Dramatic Form and Function.* Weimann
argues that this tension was *always* at work in English drama: "[T]he movement
from ritual to representation does not indicate a progressive development, but
rather defines a fundamental contradiction throughout the history of medieval and
Renaissance drama. The resolution of this contradiction took place in phases and
on various levels with changing emphases right down to the Shakespearean theater. As a matter of fact, the tensions between ritual performance and representational action which were more partially reflected in the folk play were not entirely absent from the mystery plays themselves" (58).

[16] Arnold Hauser, quoted by Jonathan Dollimore in "Two concepts of mimesis: Renaissance literary theory and *The Revenger's Tragedy*" (25). Dollimore further
observes: "The distinction between the metaphysical reality which is transcendent,
and that which is immanent, remains at the centre of Western theology and philosophy, especially in the period under discussion. It is, for example, apparent in
the Anglican-Puritan debate over the issue of exactly how divine and secular are
related" (31-32).

called into question.[17] Later, Puritans would attack the theater out-right, although the Marprelate tracts seem disturbed by a doubled set of reservations, inveighing against *Corpus Christi* dramas along with "the profane and wicked toyes of *Passion-playes*, . . . procured by Popish priests" who

> as they have transformed the celebrating of the Sacrament of the *Lord's supper* into a *Masse-game*, and all other partes of the *Ecclesiasticall service* into *theatricall sights*; so in steede of *preaching the word*, they caused it to be played.[18]

***

After Protestant reformers reinterpret the mass, the explicit displays of dumb shows would become more crucial theatrical elements. That there would be room for a dumb show in *Hamlet* is not all that surprising, anyway. Shakespeare's theater often served as a refuge for failed symbols and outmoded signs including Othello, Antony, Cleopatra, and Lear, all of whose ultimate fate is to watch them-selves acting. The eclipsing of signs animates both plot and theme of *Hamlet*, a drama which, holding "the mirror up to nature" (3.1.25), systematically teaches us to do without display. Still, the provisionality of Renaissance signs (or the need for theatrical mir-rors to catch them) is something especially hard, I think, for mod-ern audiences to recognize. For one thing, Thomas Greene claims that "[w]e are divided from most of human history" by the "incip-ient, massive, slow, uneven, almost invisible" "waning of the cere-monial sign."[19] We are divided from this history, I would add, because human history reconfigures itself in order to register this loss. But King Hamlet's fate makes even this revisionary activity impossible, when his own "real presence" becomes irrelevant to the unfolding of the Prince's play.

---

[17] Pelikan (1985) 55-56.
[18] See Jonas Barish, *The Antitheatrical Prejudice* (162-63). Sensitive to the same kind of mimetic alteration, Francis Fergusson concludes that Hamlet's "'ritual occasion' [at Elsinore] . . . is an answer to, and a substitute for, the inadequate or false rit-ual order of Denmark." See *The Idea of a Theater*. He adds: "It is in the player's scene that the peculiar theatricality of *Hamlet*–ritual as theater and theater as ritu-al; at once the lightest improvisation and the solemnest occasion–is most clearly visible" (121-22).
[19] Greene (1991) 179.

Prior to the revolutions in historiography outlined in the previous chapter, the medieval historian had for his task the providing
of a *speculum principum* or mirror for princes, a fixed compendium of
exempla which organized and interpreted political decision-making.
The historian's collection of images was both stable and self-
effacing. But increasingly in the Renaissance, historiography
becomes an activity through which its subjects instead examine
themselves. The *speculum principum* Hamlet employs in *The Murder of
Gonzago*, the mirror used to trap the conscience of the king, therefore has decidedly mixed results. Interrupting his play to announce
that the Duke's murderer is "one Lucianus, *nephew* to the *King*"
(3.2.239 *my emphasis*), Hamlet's mirror pins Claudius and also
records his own image, letting the body of his dead father slide out
of theatrical view, rendered epistemologically useless as a piece of
information.

Lacan's account of the formation of the "I" suggests there are
some mimetic strategies which allow signs to disappear, with the
result that history is not achieved by subjects so much as delegated
to them.[20] He claims that the "I" mimetically staged is jointly experienced as a specular phenomenon in opposition to "any philosophy
directly issuing from the *Cogito*."[21] Lacan explains this group production by describing how an infant's traumatic entrance into history begins with the apprehension of its image in a mirror, providing him with an enveloping awareness of his movements reflected
in the environment around him. Encountering his own "real presence," the image of himself as something external (or bound by con-
tingency) and purely accidental (or vulnerable to chance), the child
is offered the opportunity to watch himself seeing and simultaneously imagine himself disappear. This opportunity, Lacan argues,
situates the agency of the ego in a fictional direction.[22]

While Lacan concerns himself with the consequences of this arbi-
trary encounter upon the child's psyche, my interest lies more in the
effects of the "mirror stage" upon history, when it perceives its own
image as random or opportunistic. This theatrical awareness is
closely tied to a Reformation consciousness. Like the collection of
events Lacan imagines outlined in the child's mirror, Hamlet's his-

[20] Jacques Lacan, "The mirror stage as formative of the function of the I as
revealed in psychoanalytic experience."
[21] Lacan's (1977) conception of the mirror stage, he claims, sheds "light . . . on
the formation of the I as *we* experience it in psychoanalysis" (1) (*my emphasis*).
[22] Lacan (1977) 2.

tory also has very little to do with the past, completely disconnected from what has preceded it. In fact, *The Murder of Gonzago* recon-
structs history from false starts, epistemological mistakes, and
reversed roles; the "illuminative mimicry" Lacan describes is here,
as the Prince explains to Ophelia, "miching malicho" or "mischief"
(3.2.135). Hamlet invents history as a means to an end. And from
this point on, Hamlet's *Mousetrap* suggests, the patriarch's body no
longer supplies evidence–or that which postulates exactly what we
are permitted to see. If anything, that body is an optical illusion.

In the remainder of this chapter, I explore how Hamlet's
Mousetrap utilizes many of the ontological discrepancies and historical confusions which first arise in the sixteenth century. Just as history is interrupted by Hamlet's histrionic claims, the principles jointly supporting Renaissance theology, epistemology and performance
theory break apart when a new metaphysics is put into action by
Protestant reformers. The shifting images registered by Hamlet's
mirror, unrecognizable portraits like those that Descartes or
Montaigne might apprehend,[23] were especially disturbed by debates
surrounding transubstantiation. Just as King Hamlet and Claudius
appear utterly unlike to the Prince, Protestants were uncertain of
the degree to which Christ's body resembled–or was hidden by–the
communion wafer.[24] In *A Sermon preached at Paules Crosse*, the speak-
er charges Catholics with turning "Chryst out of his own likenesse,
and [making] him looke lyke a rounde cake, nothyng lyke to Iesus
Christe, no more than an apple is lyke an oyster . . . ."[25]

More telling than his indictment is the new meanings applied to
symbols along with the new pressures to read them correctly. These
changes suggest a semiotics which describe knowledge rather than
any particular state of affairs, a Renaissance epistemology which can
only and must fully know itself. This epistemology places a burden
on God, too, since He must also have a suitable image to assume
and resemble.[26]

***

---

[23] See Peter Burke, *The Renaissance Sense of the Past* (1-3, 39); and Michel
Beaujour, "Speculum, Method, and Self-Portrayal: Some Epistemological
Problems." Beaujour explores how the literary self-portraits of Montaigne,
Descartes and Bacon became progressively more acute and disruptive.

[24] In the same way, King Hamlet's once "smooth body" is now covered by a
"vile and loathsome crust" (1.5.73-74).

[25] Davies 33 n78.

[26] See Lacan (1977) 2.

Of course, certain meanings and even certain sacred bodies would be entirely lost in the mimetic space designed by Protestants, enforced by what Martin Bucer called a *ratio Christianismi*. Other bodies might find themselves hopelessly lodged between what Luther distinguished as a philosophical sign, which denoted something absent, and a theological sign, which denoted something present.[27] Posted at the opening of the play, the sentry Barnardo indicates the anxiety those distinctions could foster, baldly asking: "Who's there?" (1.1.1).[28] Still, the crucial issue in Shakespeare's play is not keeping track of lost signs but, as the ghost insists, uncovering historical conditions under which signs are forgotten. Hamlet is thus unable to turn to traditional ideas of the past for solace or even for history. Acting as "scourge and minister" and revisionist historian, the Prince instead poses subversive questions about historiography like: How extensively does trauma organize consciousness? And, given its changing makeup, what else might reasonably belong to the past?

Philip Sidney's conception of the "great passport of poetry" shares Hamlet's belief that poetry revises history in the service of an enlarged teleology, bestowing "a Cyrus upon the world [in order] to make many Cyruses."[29] More's *Utopia* relies on the same distractions, inventing a good place which answers for no place. Falstaff's theater likewise rewrites history to repair a "leaking metaphysics,"[30] extravagantly overcoming absence by manufacturing "[e]leven buckram men . . . out of/two" (2.4.214-15). The prospect that history can be refashioned or disposed of–and ontology remade or abandoned–characterizes a Renaissance imagination further extended by New World explorations, and a New World that might cope with such dissolved limits. Under these relaxed conditions, history might be written with no other reason than to let the past pass from view.

Michel de Certeau argues that Renaissance historiography was

---

[27] "Signum philosophicum est nota absentis rei, signum theologicum est nota praesentis rei." See Herman Sasse, *This is my body: Luther's contention for the Real Presence in the Sacrament of the Altar* (8, 113).

[28] Alert to such a transformation, the guard Marcellus asks Horatio the reasons for the continuous "strict and most observant watch" that "Does not divide the Sunday from the week" (1.1.79).

[29] Philip Sidney, *A Defence of Poetry* (20, 24).

[30] See Herbert Blau, *To All Appearances: Ideology and Performance* (1-2, 45).

actually attuned to the fictive possibilities Sidney describes. Sharing the "ambivalent status" of Hamlet's play (an historiography which investigates what permits history to continue), Machiavelli's *Discorsi* de Certeau argues is "in a strange situation, at once critical and fictive":

> When the historian seeks to establish, for the place of power, the rules of political conduct and the best political institutions, he *plays the role* of the prince that he is not; he analyzes what the prince *ought* to do. Such is the fiction that gives his discourse an access to the space in which it is written. Indeed, a fiction, for it is at once the discourse of the master and that of the servant . . . . The historiographer depends on 'the prince in fact,' and he produces 'the virtual prince'. . . . [But n]ever will the 'virtual prince,' a construct of discourse, be the 'prince in fact.'[31]

De Certeau's description of politics is also a parable of the theater, furnishing a history with actors rather than with agents. Shakespeare had outlined a similar state of affairs in Sonnet 94:

> They that have pow'r to hurt, and will do none,
> That do not do the thing they must do show,
> Who moving others are themselves as stone,
> Unmov'd, cold, and to temptation slow-
> They rightly do inherit heaven's graces.

The "virtual" king Claudius embodies this theatrical power most crudely, but Claudius also detects its operation throughout his court, commenting that since King Hamlet's death, "nor the exterior nor the inward man/ Resembles that it was" (2.2.6-7).

Similar ontological collisions stemmed, de Certeau claims, from European encounters with the unknown other, and European historiography emerged directly from the empirical challenge the New World posed to intelligible shapes of evidence, widening an already growing fissure between symbolic traditions and reality.[32] Like

---

[31] Michel de Certeau, *The Writing of History* (8); see also Reiss (1980) 292.
[32] See Walter Mignolo, *The Darker Side of the Renaissance: Literacy, Territoriality, and Colonization.* Mignolo claims the psychic investment drained from the centuries-old threat of Islam and transferred into the successful transatlantic expansion "invites an understanding of 'traditions' not as *something* that is there to be remembered, but the *process of remembering and forgetting* itself" (xi, xv). See also Conley's introduction to de Certeau (vii-viii); and Jacques Derrida, "The Theater of Cruelty and the Closure of Representation" (238).

Hamlet's dramaturgy, Renaissance historiography frequently choos-
es to put some evidence out of sight. But historiography must cope
with a string of mimetic failures. In response, the theater of the
Renaissance or "distracted globe" (1.5.97) will generate a fantastic
array of alibis, exempting Western bodies and corroborating a history of trauma, or history of breaks with history.[33] The new king is
especially alert to such formulations. He consoles Hamlet with the
reminder that "you must know your father lost a father,/ That
father lost, lost his" (1.2.89-90). Claudius's theory inverts history by
imagining not an original plenitude but an original loss.[34] His reading of history might also explain Herbert Blau's suggestion that "we
wouldn't need the theater if experience served us better."[35] If the
aim of Renaissance historiography is obsolescence, the aim of theater, as Blau argues, is to make itself disappear.[36]

***

[33] See Cathy Caruth, "Unclaimed Experience: Trauma and the Possibility of
History" (185); and C. John Sommerville, *The Secularization of Early Modern England*
(34).
   [34] Julia Kristeva similarly comments on Holbein's Dead Christ as a representation first imagined by Vesalius's anatomy lessons and by revenge tragedy but only
made possible by Protestant skepticism: "[A]s one looks at the dead body of this
tortured man, one cannot help asking oneself the peculiar, and interesting question: if such a corpse (and it must have been just like that) was seen by all His dis-
ciples, by His future chief apostles, by the women who followed Him, then how
could they possibly have believed, as they looked at the corpse, that that master
would rise again? Here one cannot help being struck with the idea that if death is
so terrible and if the laws of nature are so powerful, they how can they be overcome?" See "Holbein's Dead Christ."
   [35] Herbert Blau, *Take up the Bodies: Theater at the Vanishing Point* (2). Blau emphasizes how this limit creates the need for a specifically tragic theatrical experience:
"The past always needs blood donors. The theater is a means of transfusion" (9).
Like other new surveillance techniques, the Renaissance stage produces some data
that could not be fully accommodated in its discourse or epistemological schemes;
much evidence must remain–at this point–theatrical: Othello ultimately turns
Turk; Antony eventually turns statue. Philippe Lacoue-Labarthe points to some
links between Hamlet's dramaturgy and later Freudian analysis, explaining how
Freud has been read as a "pure and simple prisoner of the Western system and of
the mechanics of representation–of Graeco-Italian scenography, of classical dramaturgy, etc.–and that he had even added to its coercive power by presenting it
as a structural necessity of the human subject in general." See "Theatricum
Analyticum" (123).
   [36] For Blau (1982), "theatre is an occasion which exists most substantially in the
rehearsal of its disappearance" (xv).

This mimetic slippage becomes the subject of Hamlet's *Mousetrap*, when the Prince's script confirms the ghost's charges and indicts Claudius while rendering him victim to Hamlet's plot. Relocating metaphysics and "defying augury" (5.2.215), Hamlet attaches history to altogether different bodies. "The historical power of trauma," Cathy Caruth asserts, "is not just that the experience is repeated after its forgetting, but that it is only in and through its inherent forgetting that it is first experienced at all."[37] Baroque art forges and glorifies this disparity between personal experience and history. Describing a species of Baroque theater called *trauerspiel* (or mourning play), Walter Benjamin reads *Hamlet* as secular myth rather than tragedy precisely because it emphasizes this gap.[38] Organized by relics and around cemeteries, its courtly spectacle fastened on arrays of corpses, grieving in *Hamlet* is staged as a royal activity. Francis Barker links this grief with the production of the secular, a "figuring [of] the past as dead."[39] In the process, trauma replaces history, and a failure to experience becomes a culturally-sanctioned activity.[40] Protestant readings of the eucharist sponsor this same pathological experience.

Like Benjamin's conception of *trauerspiel*, Reiss's description of "analytical tragedy" helps account for the theatrical production of absence in *Hamlet*. Already acting "within that classification of the human (eventually due to become a general taxonomy, as Foucault has shown) which begins to be imposed at least from the beginning of the European sixteenth century," analytical tragedy is "[c]haracterized by *distance* . . . within discourse, which will now speak *of* something instead of simply speaking."[41] To be sure, a similar disruption had occurred culture-wide with the shift from oral to print culture, resulting in the creation of "discrete" languages. "[F]ar more than a mode of information diffusion," Patrick Collinson argues, the invention of print "was a mechanism for sequestering

---

[37] Caruth 187. Garber similarly suggests that *The Murder of Gonzago* resembles a "transference-neurosis" "induced as a kind of therapeutic substitution, which *can* be cured or worked on because it is present rather than lost, and because it is, in some sense, play" (320).

[38] Walter Benjamin, *The Origins of German Tragic Drama*.

[39] See Francis Barker, "Which Dead?: *Hamlet* and the ends of history." *Uses of History: Marxism, postmodernism, and the Renaissance* (55); and Roland M. Frye, "The Prince amid the Tombs." *The Renaissance Hamlet*.

[40] See Caruth 187.

[41] Reiss (1980) 4.

words from their natural habitat–sound, a humane habitat of
unforced, instructive interaction and participation."[42] To an extent,
though, print culture might "paper over" this gap by inhabiting
such limits completely, producing a surplus of texts to obscure the
"natural habitat." Hamlet will similarly use *The Mousetrap* to outline
the limits of his knowledge and to mark the extent to which he
might productively think about his thinking.[43]

But memory can disrupt metaphysical limits too. Always motivated, it always also belongs to the living.[44] James Young has argued
that memory can assume many different forms, shaped by loss,
knowledge, power or ignorance. Theatrical representation is yet
another method, although the player's rendering of Hecuba's
speech both inspires and exposes the Prince's faulty memory
(2.2.583-88). Thomas Mann suggests, however, that the epistemological problems memory introduces run even deeper:

> [T]he calling back of the dead, or the desirability of calling them
> back, was a ticklish matter, after all. At bottom, and boldly confessed,
> the desire does not exist; it is a misapprehension precisely as impos-
> sible as the thing itself, as we should soon see if nature once let it
> happen. What we call mourning for our dead is perhaps not so much
> grief at not being able to call them back as it is grief at not being
> able to want to do so.[45]

What Mann suggests is that there is no such thing as the past, only
lazy readers or bored spectators.

At the same time, bad memory can enliven theatrical performance. "Damaged, preempted, colonized as it may be," for Blau
"the subconscious can also be stubborn, with the ingenuity of amnesia[, i]n the more or less Nietzschean form of an active forgetting,
that may be making ideological claims of its own." Hamlet's version
of *The Mousetrap* incorporates the inevitable "habits, tics, giveaway

---

[42] See Collinson (1988) 121. Conley describes a simultaneous separation of
"voice, image, schema into discrete languages" (de Certeau xiv).
[43] Reiss (1980) argues that "[i]n Western history tragedy seems to have
appeared at moments that, retrospectively, are marked by a kind of 'hole' in the
passage from one dominant discourse to another. This hole, this momentary and
impossible absence of meaningfulness that is simply a necessary flaw in codification
during the process of its elaboration, will not however be filled by any law created out of tragedy. It is merely papered over, occulted" (2, 284).
[44] James E. Young, *The Texture of Memory: Holocaust Memorials and Meaning* (2).
[45] Quoted by Garber 297.

reflexes" Blau recommends actors enlist to reconstruct the "pathology of a surface."[46] Barker suggests a similar extension of theatrical technique or mimetic desire; with the shrinking or shutting down of Renaissance semiotics, he claims:

> Historical memory *becomes*, or becomes legible *as*, mourning for the 'individual' rather than for the horizon of the historicity previously established. These forms of memory, of the representation of memory–history and mourning–are engaged together in a pattern of displacement and substitution where historical memory is displaced on to and tendentially replaced by the personal version, and considerable analytic and dramatic effort is and would be then needed to unpick and demystify this dehistoricising substitution.[47]

***

There were other epistemological techniques or cognitive frameworks (methods for making pathology less superficial) that were disowned or downplayed at this time, and with them, ideas about purgatory, the saints, and the Virgin Mary. Hell even begins its slow decline.[48] What we might call a Renaissance mortuary poetics begins to take shape, as many images and ideas become less useful or less tenable, explaining less about reality, justifying little that passes for history. De Certeau similarly refers to a "mortuary circulation that produces knowledge as it concomitantly effaces itself."[49] These Renaissance mortuary poetics, morbidly preoccupied with remains and relics, organize a concept of the past that is powerful without being influential, evocative but irrelevant, something which no longer requires being thought about. A corollary to this phenomenon was a genealogical craze in which ancestry was opportunistically "forged," so that lineage, having abandoned "all trivial fond records" (*Hamlet* 1.5.99), originates where and when it is consulted.

Still another result is the diminished importance of patriarchal

---

[46] Blau (1992) describes this "pathology of a surface" (1-2).

[47] Barker (1991) 50.

[48] Horton Davies argues that: "Unquestionably the banning of the invocation of the saints . . . must have left many vacant spaces in the affections of the simple believers" (20-21).

[49] In his discussion of the "mortuary circulation" of symbolic images, de Certeau defines history as the study of the erosion of the shape of religion (see Conley xi).

bodies. In this abruptly closed semiotic system, God no longer governs the stage; if anything, he becomes another prop more or less useful for the unfolding of human texts[50] and the rabble in *Hamlet* momentarily decide to call Laertes lord (4.5.102). Christ's body is similarly lost in space, conveyed by a sign which ultimately points to itself. As Barker puts it, "[a] culture is losing its memory."[51] No wonder genealogies are so prized at this time; there is little else holding the present in place.

***

Thomas Greene describes a "profound reversal" in "human techniques of signification in the sixteenth century,"[52] a reversal made explicit when King Hamlet's body, once smooth but now encrusted and "Most lazar-like" (1.5.72), returns to the Renaissance stage encased in armor, finally insensibly and pathologically all surface.[53] This patriarchal disconnection–isolated from the world a king once organized and banished from a purgatory officially repudiated–illustrates a "general European shift in the ground of Western epistemology" at this time, a reduction or distortion of reason whose most "common theme," as Claudius reminds his nephew, is "death of fathers" (1.2.103-04).[54] This "shift [is] so basic that knowledge itself becomes constelled as a separate problem," with its own semiotics and locale.[55]

When knowledge can be isolated, it can also be lost. It is for this reason that literature absorbs philosophy in the sixteenth century, all the while expressing a newfound skepticism which results from what is increasingly experienced as the "burden of knowledge."[56]

---

[50] Eric Bentley, *The Life of the Drama* (171, 178); Derrida (1978) 239. See also Antonin Artaud, *The Theater and its Double.*

[51] Barker (1991) 48.

[52] Greene (1991) 183.

[53] I am indebted to my student Abigail Scherer for this observation. See also Caroline Walker Bynum, *The Resurrection of the Body in Western Christianity 200-1336.*

[54] Along these lines, Robert N. Watson argues that "revenge tragedy serves partly as a displacement of prayers for the dead forbidden by the Reformation." See "Giving up the Ghost: *Hamlet*, Revenge and Denial." *The Rest is Silence* (75).

[55] See Robert S. Knapp, *Shakespeare–The Theater and the Book* (8).

[56] See Cavell (1988) 179. The editors of *Mimesis: From Mirror to Method, Augustine to Descartes* (1982) argue in their introduction that: "The Erasmian or anti-Ciceronian position shifts the emphasis from universal nature to the individual nature of the reader, who is the agent of assemblage of texts into meaningful pat-

Fortunately, like the dead father who takes up space that no longer exists, what is now at stake is a vision of the world rather than the world itself. Such visions are rarely risked, moreover. Conflicting versions of the past can be supported by different texts or relegated to secluded locales–King Arthur safely spends his boyhood in Spenser's faeryland, and Eve's birth narrative comes first in *Paradise Lost*, before it can disturb her predecessor's. To prevent the fragmentation or "aggressive disintegration" that occurs when Lacan's mirror is not consulted,[57] *Utopia* puts its epistemological framework nowhere. We see this problem (and solution) of the "real presence" also located in the transubstantiated bread and wine.

Yet another example of a closed semiotic system is my first example, Hamlet's *Mousetrap*. The Prince not only uses the players to replicate his uncle's crime, but simultaneously alters those murderous events and meanings. While Hamlet's play functions as a sign, then, its reference is ultimately unclear. Is it a way to sting Claudius's guilty conscience or to inform Hamlet of what the Prince does not already know? The first possibility seems less likely, even if *The Murder of Gonzago* prompts Claudius's guilt when afterwards the king tries to pray, stimulated by remorse. At the same time, Claudius reads the semiotic system of his body as a key to the implacability of his conscience (3.3.36-70). He commands: "Bow, stubborn knees, and heart with strings of steel," only to lament: "My words fly up, my thoughts remain below" (3.3.70; 97).[58] Claudius exemplifies the problem many Protestants wrestled with:

terns" (13). Beaujour similarly notes how "the epistemological revolution of Renaissance science can be read–at least on one level–as an elaboration of new methods conferring upon the individual scientist as philosopher a personal responsibility for his inferences, and for testing–logically or experimentally–their validity" (189).

[57] There are a number of other accounts of Renaissance pathology. See, for instance, Watson, who claims that: "Hamlet's father, already regurgitated by his tome (1.4.50-51), becomes all too model a Host at this mixed sacrament . . . " (83). Sommerville likewise describes how "Protestantism shifted the emphasis toward a directed history, from the sacramentalism of a religious culture toward a pilgrim's faith. Protestants even redefined the sacraments, as remainders–and therefore historical–rather than reenactments" (34). Most explicitly, Lacan (1977) defines the "lines of fragilization" that define the "anatomy of phantasy": "This fragmented body . . . appears in the form of disjointed limbs, or of those organs represented in exoscopy . . . the very same that the visionary Hieronymus Bosch has fixed, for all time, in painting" (4-5).

[58] William Engel's study, *Mapping Mortality: The Persistence of Memory and Melancholy in Early Modern England* argues for a "mnemonically oriented principle of aesthetics" at this time (3).

How can a sign be mnemonic if it does not belong to the originary
object?

Rather than addressing Claudius's dilemma, Hamlet's *Mousetrap*
supplies the Prince with knowledge to which he otherwise lacks
access, not raw data but awareness of philosophical limits, not
insight (something provided when the mirror is turned up to
Gertrude),[59] but recognition of the phantoms that dominate him.
This is the kind of knowledge which Reiss calls "impossible" or
"unthinkable,"[60] and through it is created a past, like the armored
dead king, no longer susceptible to or assailable by humanist scholarship, Catholic dogmatism or Protestant reform. A history without
a subject,[61] it resembles Polonius's description of the players' repertory, which includes "tragedy, comedy, history, pastoral, pastoral-
comical, historical-pastoral, tragical-historical, tragical-comical-his-
torical-pastoral, scene individable, or poem unlimited" (2.2.392-96).
Such an artifact hermetically sealed belongs completely to the uses
to which it can be put, as Fortinbras quickly learns. He arrives in
Denmark, surveys the array of bodies on stage, and concludes that
he has "some rights of memory in this kingdom" (5.2.394).

What Fortinbras realizes immediately is something Greene must
remind us of, that the crisis which confronted "communal, perfor-
mative signs" in the sixteenth century "did not signal any decline in
the frequency of ceremonies . . . . Arguably, in statistical terms, the
sixteenth century provided more ritual and ceremonial occasions
than any other century."[62] But Protestant signs function precisely
because cognitive pathways have been blocked or rerouted; they
occupy space where the grounds for comparison, reference or interpretation have been shut down. The semiotic replacement Hamlet

---

[59] For Gertrude's development, see Lacan (1977), especially his discussion of
how a *Gestalt* is capable of formative effects, including that of sexual maturation (2-
3).

[60] Reiss (1980) argues that: "Tragedy appears ultimately as the discourse that
groups and encloses a certain 'absence of signification' that may well be common
to all discursive acts at the 'inception' of the discourse making such acts possible,
and that renders *im*possible, before such particular ordering, the meaningfulness of
any such discourse" (3).

[61] Blau (1992) 3. Some critics have made the case that the play provides a version of Martin Luther's life: Wittenberg, after all, was Luther's stronghold. Among
the most compelling arguments that Luther was a "prototype" for the Prince is
Waddington's "Lutheran *Hamlet*." See also Matheson 391. Benjamin notes that the
great German dramatists of the baroque era were Lutherans (138).

[62] Greene (1991) 182, 195

proposes and Fortinbras eventually provides therefore differs from the script Othello authors with Iago. Othello has no faith in Desdemona's love or cannot know it for himself, but Hamlet does not care about knowing.

In fact, if planned to confirm his suspicions, Hamlet's *Mousetrap* stirs new ones, and the epistemological results of his play-within-a-play not only confuse him but us. Part of the anxiety plaguing Hamlet, as Robert N. Watson argues, is worrying "what if the lost father proves not to be a ghost, but instead a skull; not the victim of extraordinary villainy, but of ordinary decay?"[63] Hamlet's solution to these fears is to construct an "eternal blazon" (1.5.21) which merely obeys Horatio's command to the ghost to "Stay, illusion" (1.1.130). His staging provides the "fantasy of an uninterrupted present,"[64] a mimetic fantasy also indulged when Luther's colleague Johannes Forster writes a Hebrew dictionary devoid of rabbinic commentary.[65] These fantasies are further shared by reformers who attack the Catholic doctrine of transubstantiation. Under Protestant scrutiny, Christ's corporeal qualities become inconsequential, secondary, irrelevant: his physical attributes, in other words, block informed knowing and interrupt sacred memory.

***

Supplied by Hamlet's theater and the eucharistic feast alike are a set of mimetic doubles or plays-within-plays, a pot-luck philosophy where the father's body is permitted to slip away and the past enabled to slide out of view, finally free of the present. The power of such mimetic strategies now lies in their insufficiency, as Nicholas Ridley explains in a *Brief Declaration of the Lord's Supper* (1544). Ridley denies that he reduced the mass to a "bare signe or figure" which represented Christ, "none otherwise than the Ivy Bush doth represent the wine in a tavern, or as a vile person gorgeously apparelled may represent a king or a prince in a play."[66]

---

[63] Watson 76.

[64] Blau, *Blooded Thought: Occasions of Theatre* (xv). Lacan (1977) compares this invention to the monkey's encounter with a mirror, where the monkey masters the image by finding it empty (1).

[65] See Friedman.

[66] Quoted by Davies 104. This new, improved stage also resembles the "non-theological space" Derrida (1978) claims is produced by Artaud's "theater of cru-

Instead, Ridley implies, Reformation Christianity has simply become more adept at imitating imitation and manufacturing optical illusions, producing vernacular bibles, envisioning laity doubling for priests, building communion tables to replace sacrificial altars, supplying an "orthopaedic totality" that stands in for broken Catholic signs.[67] It is because the Prince is so sensitive to the quality of these substitutions that Hamlet warns the players about merely overdoing special effects and "out-Heroding Herod" (3.2.14). Marx will likewise remind us to distinguish "the steady forward motion of the mode of real philosophical knowledge from the talkative, exoteric, variously gesticulating phenomenological consciousness of its subject."[68] Protestant mimesis not only threatens this world but the next, and Benjamin predicts that eschatology will vanish in its closed semiotic system (or hall of mirrors) which illuminates–and guarantees–that nothing can be transubstantiated. "The hereafter is emptied of everything which contains the slightest breath of this world," Benjamin suggests, "in order to clear an ultimate heaven, enabling it, as a vacuum, one day to destroy the world with catastrophic violence."[69]

But the recommended solutions to this threat, at least in the sixteenth century, remain theatrical. The Tridentine revisions outlined by the Papacy roundly criticize irreverence at the celebration of the mass by ignorant priests. The Council fathers "observed that sincerity was of great importance, and . . . criticised those who pro-

---

elty" when it expelled God from the stage. Derrida maintains: "There is always a murder at the origin of cruelty, the necessity named cruelty. And, first of all, a parricide. The origin of theater, such as it must be restored, is the hand lifted against the abusive wielder of the logos, against the father, against the God of a stage subjugated to the power of speech and text" (235, 239).

Indeed, Hamlet's production, especially the dumb show, accords rather precisely with the techniques outlined in Artaud's manifesto for a "Theater of Cruelty." The manifesto contains a list of plays to be staged, including "[w]orks from the Elizabethan theater stripped of their text and retaining only the accouterments of period, situations, characters, and action" (100).

[67] See Lacan (1977) 4.

[68] Quoted by Blumenberg (1986) 119, 142.

[69] In his introduction to Benjamin's *Origin of German Tragic Drama*, George Steiner notes that the antecedents of German baroque theater were located "not in the classics, but in the medieval misreading of classical-Senecan fragments and in the obsessive 'physicality' of the mystery cycles." Benjamin, who discusses the Herodian dramas at length in his account of *trauerspiel*, notes: "At the moment when the ruler indulges in the most violent displays of power . . . . [b]oth history and the higher power, which checks its vicissitudes, are recognized as manifest in him" (66, 70).

nounced the sacred words like actors on a stage; it was recommended that celebrants speak gravely and clearly."[70] The trick, as
Hamlet learns when he offers Claudius up as both criminal and victim, is to make imitation less shoddy, more substantial. His praise
of the player-king's speech, before "never acted," almost crudely
lists its satisfactions: it is "caviare to the general," "an excellent play,
well digested in the scenes," and not "savoury" but "wholesome as
sweet" (2.2.33-41).

***

Hans Blumenberg suggests that reason was forced into an intellectual detour when made to answer questions only transcendental systems could pose, deluding itself that, like Herod, it might manage
its vast ambitions. Christianity, in contrast, "arose from a self-sur-
render, in that it equipped itself with a theology only when it wanted to make itself possible in a world that, strictly speaking, it
denied."[71] Protestantism will push this capitulation even further,
when it sees Christ's body and blood first and last as bread and
wine. Literally theatricalizing the loss of signs, Christianity imitates
its own pathology.[72] Situating itself in a world it struggles to deny,
Hamlet's stagecraft similarly yields to mimesis and accommodates
illusions it seeks to expose. Employing a new range of untransubstantiated signs, the play-within-a-play out Hamlets Hamlet.

Repeatedly, Shakespeare's audience is asked to educate itself
about Renaissance pathology, to continually revise its "sense of
what is happening, even at the most basic level of whether a body
is alive or dead."[73] This seems clear in *1 Henry IV*, where the battle
at Shrewsbury is waged by a multiplicity of kings and Falstaff
returns from the dead to kill the slain Hotspur. But Shakespeare's
theater also provides us with an assembly-line manufacture of props

---

[70] Davies 142.

[71] Blumenberg (1986) 119.

[72] According to Gunter Gebauer and Christoph Wulf, "Every historical period
is . . . a 'double;' conditions prior to its sense of its own beginning tend to be forgotten in favor of emphasis on uniqueness and originality." See *Mimesis: Culture-Art-
Society* (76). The Reformation's mimetic strategy is to repress itself: it duplicates its
origin precisely by obscuring historical change.

[73] Brian Gibbons, *Shakespeare and Multiplicity* (68).

like Othello's handkerchief, signs of "bad remembering"[74] which
guarantee history by plugging metaphysics.[75]

Moreover, within the greatly-expanded confines of Renaissance
theater, the foreign bodies of Turks or New World bodies of slaves
become casualties of mimetic slippage and open, like Laertes, to the
false charge of "incontinency" (2.1.30). These bodies are not spared
by Western alibis but made to substantiate them.[76] A metaphysics
which firmly attaches itself to such bodies, coupled with a historiography that repeatedly denies them, is also what allows Islam to
finally become less of a military and religious threat during the
Renaissance, and to function instead as a double for the papacy or
for the Lutherans, exposing them not to charges of heresy but
duplicity. Formerly inspiring apocalyptic terror, Mahomet becomes
interchangeable with the puppets or "mammets" increasingly found
on Renaissance stages.[77] Even Luther's image becomes graphically
distorted.[78] We might see such dislocated images as neurotic adjust-

---

[74] Barker (1991) 50.

[75] An excellent discussion of the image of multiplying Turks in *1 Henry IV* is
provided by Richard Hillman, "'Not Amurath an Amurath Succeeds': Playing
Doubles in Shakespeare's *Henriad*." Hillman argues that "the cultural projection
that goes with the name Amurath is detached from historical specificity, freed to
resonate among and between particular bearers of it." "The *Henriad* constructs–and
deconstructs–its central figure through a complex network of matches" (161-62).
And, in *Othello*, Hillman notes, "the Turks appear as antagonists at once concrete
and shadowy, hard to pin down as they feint toward Rhodes, then make for
Cyprus" (182). It is interesting that even while the image of multiplying Turks ter-
rorized Europe, Sidney could hold out the specter of "many Cyruses" as something
beneficial.

[76] We seem to be returning to these concerns with the intense interest in
Clinton aide Vincent Foster's misplaced body, or in the renewed valorization of
the bodies of dead Presidents thanks, at least in part, to filmmaker Oliver Stone.
Also see the full page ad in *The New York Times* (Jan 29 1995; Section A:16) fund-
ed by the "Western Journalism Center," which lists bodily "inconsistences" under
various headings. Apparently, watching the video available for purchase will solve
the problem–the specular phenomenon Lacan describes once again at odds with
any "cogito."

[77] Scott Cutler Shershow investigates Renaissance puppets or mammets as a
corruption of the name "Mohamet" in "'The Mouth of 'hem All': Ben Jonson,
Authorship, and the Performing Object" (196 n30). Shershow's history usefully discusses puppets as unruly objects in the theater of the West. See also C.A. Patrides,
who describes the diminution of the Muslim threat in "'The Bloody and Cruell
Turke': the Background of a Renaissance Commonplace."

[78] Part of what I am investigating in this chapter is why the English debt to
Luther is so unclear. See William A. Clebsch, "The Elizabethans on Luther."
Clebsch claims that: "The spirit of Luther's religion and theology began to settle
on Elizabethan England like a London fog; hauntingly unspecifiable, and with real
welcome only after his death, it just seeped into the atmosphere. Few, indeed, knew

6. Peder Trellund, Altar stand for Hojbjerg Church (c. 1586). Holy images are now replaced by texts, with the result that the past becomes at once a sacred source, historical model, and aesthetic object. Trellund, a schoolmaster, gave King Frederik II the altarpiece in 1586. The etchings consist of quotations from the Bible and authors like Horace and Vives.

ments to the trauma of the Renaissance.[79] Hamlet will simply call these images "food for worms" (4.3.19-28).

Conclusion

This Renaissance trauma inspires other responses, like an icono-clasm which destroys images because what they signalled could not be moved or emptied out. Such sympathies (or tensions) are record-ed in the Hojbjerg altar stand by schoolmaster and calligrapher Peder Trellund (illustration 6), and in the Thorslunde altarpiece (illustration 7). Each image depicts the contest between "dominant" and "occulted" discourses that Reiss describes. But within each work the perspective continually shifts, so that the eye (or imagina-tion) has no place to rest: neither side adequately translates the other. As a result, it is difficult to make out exactly which sacred signs are being valorized and which are being discounted, even if, for instance, the Catholic mass is clearly caricatured in the Thorslunde altarpiece. Because Protestant memory is mimetic, its "dominant theoretical model" is premised on and clarified by the "dominant occulted practice."[80] But both kinds of signs in each image are manageable as a set of optical illusions like the out-Heroded Herod, meaningful only when they are meaningless.

When memory becomes untenable as an intellectual construct, reason must assume its place as part of an "analytico-referential" discourse, comprised of disembodied signs like Yorick's skull or the communion wafer, signs that do not govern or structure or even refer to actuality. Reformation epistemology thus creates a richly textured and aggressively horizontal space, so that the real problem plaguing Hamlet, according to Barker, is figuring out: "Which dead?" or, more simply: Which bodies belong to the past? To be sure, that difficulty becomes even more pressing with the abolition of purgatory. A now-equally urgent question, and one we ask of the Thorslunde altarpiece, is: Which bodies belong to the present?

---

exactly whence it sprang, or, for that matter, precisely what it was" (116). Cf. Basil Hall, who describes a more arid climate, arguing that "English protestants . . . were willing to accept gladly Luther's theological aid in attacking Catholicism while on the whole discarding his sacramental teaching." "The Early Rise and Gradual Decline of Lutheranism in England 1520-1600" (104).

[79] Derrida (1978) 244.
[80] See Reiss (1982) 11.

7. Altarpiece for Thorslunde Church (1561). The artist is unknown, but the painting is a copy of a propaganda print by Lucas Cranach the Younger from 1546, where Luther occupies the pulpit. The altar front depicts the three most important elements of the Lutheran service: baptism without immersion; communion in the form of both bread and wine; and a bare altar, save for crucifix and candles. The image also offers a caricature of the Catholic mass, and thus registers two conflicting images or stances: sacred history is not to be revised but opposed.

Perhaps it is this greatly-expanded theatrical arena that historian Steven Ozment bemoans, contending that the Reformation was a failure because it did not succeed in installing any new kind of discourse.[81] I would instead suggest that the Reformation commemorates this failure through a new discourse of untransubstantiated hosts, elements of a "lost semiotics"[82] like "dead man's fingers," rotting skulls or "mildew'd ears," furnishing a less alien and more complete structure of signs for a ghostly world. In such a world, nothing reminds us of anything, not even apples of oranges or, as the case may be, of oysters.

---

[81] Steven Ozment, *The Age of Reform 1250-1550: An Intellectual and Religious History of Late Medieval and Reformation Europe*: "The Reformation did not reform the whole church, much less European society, and well before midcentury it needed reform itself" (434). See also Reiss (1982) 106.

[82] I borrow this phrase from Greene (1991), who describes a space "still saturated with formal performed signs but no longer, at all levels, presenting them as determinant" (196).

CONCLUSION

THE ARITHMETIC OF MEMORY :
RELICS, REMAINS, AND FAERY LITTER

I have proposed that a number of ways were devised to take stock of the semiotic spoils and failed signs that came to litter the Renaissance imagination, a variety of techniques for mapping Reformation promises or pathology. What emerged was an entirely different method for keeping track of lost or depleted signs, a mnemonic scheme that concerned itself less with a symbol s moral weight or theological value. Perhaps this was because the power of knowing was now instead tied to counting.[1] Along with developments in trade and commerce, language was gradually replaced by mathematics as a tool of discovery. Indeed, many of the investigations into the human sciences that Foucault describes were made possible by a symbolic language that no longer pretends to signify or create, that no longer performs an organic role, but merely serves as a notational or accounting device.

Without language s Orphic function, there is no longer the same effort to reconcile the universe or recall divine winds; all of these longings have vanished, or been codified by literature, so that Milton describes a paradise that is lost. In the same way, Renaissance musicology becomes less attuned to cosmological harmonies, more interested in its quantitative effects.[2] This shift had begun earlier, however, and under official auspices when—as if recognizing how the value of sacred symbols really accrued—the House of Commons petitioned in 1532 to reduce the number of holy days.[3] But the dimensions of this shift dramatically widen as its ambitions move outside state offices. If mathematics teaches poets about the stars, politicians about war, physicists about celestial bodies, we are now inhabiting a universe of allegorical debris, ghosts, and faery litter. A very different system of figuration has taken

---

[1] See Reiss, *Knowledge, Discovery and Imagination in Early Modern Europe* (1997); and Cynthia Hay, ed. *Mathematics from Manuscript to Print.*
[2] See Reiss 136.
[3] Somerville 34.

shape, more sensitive to signs that have lost their value and capacious enough for these dead ends.

***

No poet is as shrewd as Spenser is to the vital power of cultural decay, or as adept at tabulating sacred remains. One model for these poetics is provided for us briefly at Mount Acidale, towards the close of Book 6 of *The Faerie Queene*, when Colin Clout summons a hundred and four maidens with his pipe. But the knight Calidore stumbles upon them and breaks their circle open, destroying an hermetically-sealed but fragile space, forever dividing sacred inspiration from the poet s song. We are given another model for the New Poet, however, in the figure of Despair, who takes his turn at writing the Protestant history recorded in Spenser s poem towards the close of Book 1. Explaining to Redcrosse Knight that the most successful chivalric quests are rewarded in hell (1.9.43), Despair quickly realizes that the knight will be an easy target and proceeds to elaborate his case more graphically, showing him painted in a table plaine,/ The damned ghosts, that doe in torments waile,/ And thousand feends that doe them endlesse paine/ With fire and brimstone, which for euer shall remaine (1.9.49.6-9). Not only are the torments of hell permanent, but Despair s table records them perfectly. Spenser s allegory has become a mortuary poetic, an uncomplicated conception of how things finish, and where they end.

Particularly intriguing is the way all preceding chivalric narratives ultimately resemble each other in Despair s eschatology. No extenuating circumstances alter final reckonings, all myths are finally interred. Susanne Wofford points to the infinite possibility of prior narratives in *The Faerie Queene*, the set of origins behind every figure which Spenser s allegory both generously evokes and painstakingly avoids. How different is the genealogy for the figures of Adam and Eve that Milton will propose, an origin always countered by an ideal.[4] The pair, as the angel Raphael suggests, might eventually ascend to heaven, their bodies ultimately absorbed by Eden. How different, too, is the mangled shadow of Antony, a tragic remainder or failed host whom Shakespeare cannot dispose

---

[4] Susanne Wofford, *The Choice of Achilles: The Ideology of Figure in the Epic* (299).

of adequately or completely, his hero a set of sacred remains that Catholicism had once been able to extinguish altogether.

What for Milton or Shakespeare constitutes celestial litter for Spenser forms the elementary particles of both earthly and heavenly existence, building blocks of desire forever housed in a seminary of lively form, a luminous showcase for mutability. These remains are ancestral rather than consequential; living archetypes never fully discarded, they inspire and transpire rather than clog or restrain.[5] Yet Despair s table provides a clear if gruesome picture of end results. Augury can neither be ignored nor defied in Spenser s universe, its explanatory power always in fact increasing. Such a science of (or emanating from) the dead inspires the machinery behind the characters and events and images of Spenser s poem.

***

Given augury s enormous explanatory value, the Catholic doctrine of transubstantiation (which suggests that sacred symbols *only* have an afterlife) is an impossible and not merely anachronistic concept in *The Faerie Queene*. As I have tried to detail in this book, the world outside Spenser s poem increasingly agreed. Although medieval reformers themselves had argued over the terminology of transubstantiation, the nature of the evidence—the status of the bread and wine—was never itself debated, prior to Reformation disputes. Even Lollards consented that the mass was a sacrifice in which Christ s actual body and blood were consumed. There were no sacred remains, no Catholic relics.

But the Reformation imagination produced a wealth of ruins, Luther s views about transubstantiation sometimes dismantling his own earlier stances.[6] Catholic John Lechmere seems to recognize the way this Protestant imagining works, cleverly defending his

---

[5] See Harry Berger, Jr. (1988) 164. Describing the poem s anatomizing of the powers and methods of allegory, Wofford notes, in contrast, that [w]hile many of Ovid s metamorphoses seem to provide a genuine release or escape into a consoling natural world, Spenser s more often are punishments or markers, symbolic milestones commemorating losses . . . (300).

[6] Margaret Aston writes that Reformation England acquired a whole suite of ruins in English Ruins and English History: The Dissolution and the Sense of the Past (231). Aston also emphasizes that the English literary and historical imagination was affected more by ecclesiastical ruins (e.g. monastic lands or destroyed church plate) than by secular Roman ruins (at Bath, for example).

Church s reading of the eucharist. In a treatise on the real presence issued in 1635, Lechmere asserts,

> how easilie in the heate of your passion, you bring a *man* . . . to almost nothing . . . . you first . . . laugh at the *man*, and then begin to dispoile him of his *definition* . . . . He is mangled enough, now, one would think; having neither eies, nor hands, nor eares: you have made of him a lump of earth, *quid quantum & colaratum.* one blow more and you may beat him into dust. but that will not satisfie your rage; you turne him thus disfigured, this *quantum & coloratum* into a meere shape or *picture* that he may be without sustance: and then you stab him through, with an *Ecce homo Iesuiticus*; wherewith you fixe him to the paper, where he hanges . . . till he be torne out, to light *tobacco*, and so turned into smoke.[7]

Although Lechmere construes Protestant impulses as not reforming but horribly destructive, he nonetheless imagines a transcendental solution, a divine ascent, so that these celestial cast-offs finally make their way heavenward. In contrast, Despair seeks to turn Spenser s poem into a heap of ashes, something for Milton s devils to feast upon perennially.

***

Maurice Powicke maintains that the most heated religious debates in sixteenth-century England were barely occupied with doctrinal issues. The English Reformation was instead, he claims, an act of state, a political rather than theological procedure.[8] During Henry s reign at least, the country was in basic agreement: there were no Protestant dissenters or Catholic recusants; the only people burned, Powicke says, were a few mad heretics or traitors, the casualties far fewer or less symbolic than Lechmere s graphic account suggests. As is well known, Powicke argues,

> formal continuity was maintained in England to a degree without parallel in any other reformed country with the exception of Sweden. Episcopal government, the assembly of the clergy in convocation and synods, the general diocesan system, the method of exercising disci-

---

[7] Lechmere 279.

[8] Maurice Powicke, *The Reformation in England* (1). See also Alister E. McGrath, *Reformation Thought: an Introduction.* Horton Davies similarly claims that Reformation England had no theologians (5).

pline, and for twenty years the rites and ceremonies which had devel-
oped in the past to give expression to the doctrine of the Church, all
these were retained.[9]

Still, one might ask whether the apparent irrelevance or absence of
theological issues was not itself a theological issue or even a forceful theological stance. For critics like John Guillory, the Renaissance
imagination takes up precisely where sacred inspiration leaves off,
so that continuity or tradition—as Powicke also claims—now becomes
a basic principle of belief.[10] For the authors I have explored here,
a better question thus might be: How does this continuity work?
Does the Reformation air simply get thinner, or does Redcrosse s
elevated view of the New Jerusalem gradually recede? Despair offers
a worst-case scenario of secular rereadings, but Spenser will continually experiment with the limits of inspiration, repeatedly posing
to us another question: What are relics relics of?

Of course, there were efforts besides Spenser s to preserve
corpses or to make rotting signs make sense. Coinciding with
Elizabeth s death in 1603, the city of London began to track deaths
and births in weekly records called *Bills of Mortality*. These statistics
were primarily used by merchants to predict how many clients
would leave the city during times of plague. A notions merchant
named John Graunt, in his *Natural and Political Observations . . . upon
the Bills of Mortality* (1662), examined these records for the years
between 1604 and 1661 and prepared a set of tables about the
dead, detailing differences between men and women, countryfolk
and city-dwellers.[11] Graunt s augury did not convert the bodies of
the dead but simply counted them, collecting signs which manifest-
ly did not mean.[12]

---

[9] Powicke 37.

[10] Guillory viii.

[11] Graunt also aimed to to know how many people there be of each Sex, State,
Age, Religious, Trade, Rank, or Degree, etc. by the knowing whereof Trade and
Government may be made more certain, and Regular; for, if men know the People
as aforesaid, they might know the consumption they would make, so as Trade
might not be hoped for when it is impossible. See Peter L. Bernstein s discussion
in *Against the Gods: The Remarkable Story of Risk*. I am grateful to James Picerno for
directing me to Bernstein s work.

[12] Philip Kreager provides an interesting reading of Graunt s work in New
Light on Graunt (129). Dan Sperber might have us read all signs as Graunt does.
 When we strip the work of Levi-Strauss of the semiological burden with which he
has chosen to encumber it, Sperber writes, we will then realise that he was the

Graunt s reading of remains resembles a number of imaginative withdrawals in *The Faerie Queene*. If Redcrosse learns his heavenly fate at the end of Book 1, what s unusual is not this knowledge itself, but how little it accords with his current status or beliefs. The knight s experience has little impact on its ends. Similarly, the brief accounts Graunt examined, like the postmortem statistics Despair records, deface greater grace [13] and point to the secular invention of a   neutral   pathless world. [14] If allegory basically treats the world as a collection of accidents, in 1637 Lloyd s of London also sets up shop, and England s insurance industry, crudely begun a half-century earlier with guarantees for sea cargo against poor weather or ruthless pirates, becomes a keen competitor.[15]

Confusing demographics and conflicting mortality rates swell the data of Spenser s poem, and Guyon and the palmer often find themselves busy burying bodies and making funeral arrangements. This activity also underlies the sixteenth-century invention of algebra, for which it appears less important to know what symbols mean; the real task, as Arthur learns with the diseased knight Maleger (2.11), is figuring out how to dispose of them. In this encounter, the Prince must not only drain a Herculean myth of its force, but crush the empty container.[16] Yet Arthur s work of disenchantment is Despair s sorry task too. Urging Redcrosse to cut his losses, Despair may have single-handedly prompted actuarial science, calculating the odds that fates worse than death await even the goodliest knights.[17] His calculus of the sacred ignores the mystery of second chances, something that seems to hold Spenser s

first to propose the fundamentals of an analysis of symbolism which was finally freed from the absurd idea that symbols mean. See *Rethinking Symbolism* (84). Yet this kind of analysis seems to be at work in Spenser s poem; Wofford notes that frequently the presence of the [allegorical] figure requires the absence of the person, an absence often marked at the level of the fiction by a suppressed death (299).

[13] See Nohrnberg 203.
[14] Somerville 18, 34.
[15] See Charles Wright and C. Ernest Fayle, *A History of Lloyd's: From the Founding of Lloyd's Coffee House to the Present Day*.
[16] For a discussion of such myths of disenchantment, see Gross (11-12, 19-20).
[17] D. Keith Thomas refers to this development in *Religion and the Decline of Magic*, which is cited by Lorraine J. Daston, The Domestication of Risk: Mathematical Probability and Insurance 1650-1830 (244). Another reading of this data is offered by Engels (1995), who argues that the mapping of mortality is a focal purpose and animating impulse of Renaissance metaphorics (3). See also Nohrnberg 152-53.

poem together. Despair is an underwriter, an early-modern Kevorkian, reducing all stories to their ends.

**

Graunt s assembly of statistics coincides with the Renaissance col-lection and disposal of sacred remains I have been examining here. In so much poetry of the period lies a fascination with incalcitrant data that would subvert transubstantiation, like Spenser s hoggish Grill, who refuses to be accommodated in providential schemes or made responsible to human wishes. Christ s body and blood like-wise become too holy to actualize themselves through any human science. Calculus and algebra emerge to deal with this new evidence of failure, supplying the arithmetic of memory Hamlet describes (5.2.114) and furnishing a neat discourse of dislocated signs.[18] Spenser s Giant will import these signs wholesale into the Legend of Justice. But, like Graunt s calculus, such a mortuary poetics produces rather than represents knowledge in order to evade the imaginative scandal left behind by decaying signs, the moral trap Despair inhabits. Like the information Graunt derives from the bodies of the dead, this is knowledge wrested from the demise of inspiration, extracted from the failure of memory.

Protestant theology fashions and protects itself with these unwieldy or broken signs which somehow continue to radiantly mean. It is for this reason, Blumenberg explains, that myths not only outlast Enlightenment thinking but are closely entwined with it.[19] If myths help humans stand their ground against the gods, Blumenberg claims there arises more air for human lungs and more ground for myth to cover, more phantoms then necessary. Eventually nothing remains but remains. Sixteenth-century debates

----

[18] Much later than the appearance of zero is the invention of a notation for shifting signs. The signs + and - are recorded in the 1540 *Grounde of Artes* by Englishman Robert Record; and the 1557 *Whetstone of Witte* introduces =. Brian Rotman argues that the zero sign, in contrast, first appears in the thirteenth cen-tury; see *Signifying Nothing: The Semiotics of Zero* (1). Rotman links the introduction of zero to the invention of the vanishing point in perspective art and of imaginary money in economic exchange, all necessary advances, I would argue, for develop-ments in the insurance trade, especially for its initial projects like the selling of life-time annuities to healthy children.

[19] Blumenberg (1985) points to the persistent reworking of the Faust legend by Marlowe, Goethe, and Mann.

over transubstantiation momentarily endanger those phantoms, but new myths are quickly elaborated in their place: if the once-legendary Hell is now declining, Luther s devil seems busier and more destructive.[20] At the same time, Renaissance mythmaking also becomes bracketed, less ambitious, a neat set of allegorical dead-ends. If *The Faerie Queene* is ultimately a dream belonging to Arthur, it only comes alive when he sleeps.

Arthur is not the only spoil, for Spenser s faeryland is a world heaped with broken machinery like Acrasia s ruined Bower or Busirane s burnt temple and the now-vacant circle surrounding Colin Clout. It is cluttered by signs and symbols that belong to no one, resist meaning, and fail to clarify the world that evokes them. The architecture of this collapsed imagination is pictured by Alma s Castle, reduced to a set of mathematical formulas and timeless numbers, a closed system unable even to reproduce itself. At once a greedie graue, battleground, dreamscape, and hospitale, Spenser s faeryland becomes a universe that is permanently temporary, a world of fictions—much like our own—which can never be redeemed or dissolved.

---

[20] Luther s tracts mention the devil more than Christ. Gross s account may explain the phenomenon: stark tropes of apocalyptic personification are concentrated into a few ultimate symbols—Beast, Whore, Antichrist. Even within a largely demystified, skeptical discourse on idolatry, one that reflects no apparent belief in literal demons, some residue of a more primitive ambivalence tends to reassert itself (37).

BIBLIOGRAPHY

Allen, William. *A Defense and Declaration of the Catholike Churchies Doctrine Touching Purgatory. English Recusant Literature 1558-1640. Vol. 18.* ed. D.M. Rogers (London: The Scolar Press, 1970).

————. *A True, Sincere, and Modest Defense of English Catholics.* (London, 1584).

Alter, Robert and Frank Kermode, ed. *The Literary Guide to the Bible.* (Cambridge, MA: Harvard University Press, 1987).

Anderson, Benedict. *Imagined Communities: Reflections on the Origin and Spread of Nationalism.* (rev. ed.) (NY: Verso, 1991).

Anderson, Judith. "The Antiquities of Fairyland and Ireland." *Journal of English and Germanic Philology* (April 1987) 199-214.

Artaud, Antonin. *The Theater and its Double.* trans. Mary Caroline Richards (NY: Grove Press, 1958).

Aston, Margaret. "English Ruins and English History: The Dissolution and the Sense of the Past." *Journal of the Warburg and Courtauld Institutes* 36 (1973) 231-55.

Attridge, Derek, Geoff Bennington and Robert Young (eds.) *Post-Structuralism and the question of history.* (NY: Cambridge University Press, 1987).

Bakan, David. *Sigmund Freud and the Jewish Mystical Tradition* (Princeton, NJ: D. Van Nostrand Company, Inc., 1958).

Barker, Francis. "Which dead?: *Hamlet* and the ends of history." *Uses of History: Marxism, postmodernism, and the Renaissance.* ed. Francis Barker, et al. (NY: St. Martin's Press, 1991) 47-75.

Barish, Jonas. *The Antitheatrical Prejudice.* (Berkeley: University of California Press, 1981).

Bartels, Emily. *Spectacles of Strangeness: Imperialism, Alienation, and Marlowe.* (Philadelphia: University of Pennsylvania Press, 1993).

Beajour, Michel. "Speculum, Method, and Self-Portrayal: Some Epistemological Problems." *Mimesis: From Mirror to Method, Augustine to Descartes.* ed. John D. Lyons and Stephen G. Nichols, Jr. (Hanover, NH: University Press of New England, 1982) 188-96.

Beilin, Elaine. "Elizabeth Cary and *The Tragedie of Mariam.*" *Papers on Language and Literature* 16, 1 (1980) 45-64.

Beitchman, Philip. "Milton and Cabala, Reconsidered" (unpublished essay).

Bellamy, Elizabeth. "The Vocative and the Vocational: The Unreadability of Elizabeth in *The Faerie Queene.*" *ELH: English Literary History* 54, 1 (1987) 1-30.

————. *Translations of Power: Narcissism and the Unconscious in Epic History.* (Ithaca: Cornell University Press, 1992).

Benjamin, Walter. *The Origin of German Tragic Drama.* trans. John Osborne. introduction by George Steiner. (NY: Verso, 1985).

Bentley, Eric. *The Life of the Drama.* (NY: Applause Theatre Book Publishers, 1991).

Berger, Harry, Jr. *The Allegorical Temper: Vision and Reality in Book II of Spenser's Faerie Queene*. (New Haven: Yale University Press, 1957).

———. *Revisionary Play: Studies in the Spenserian Dynamics*. (Berkeley: University of California Press, 1988).

———. *Second World and Green World: Studies in Renaissance Fiction-Making*. (Berkeley: University of California Press, 1988).

Bernal, Martin. *Black Athena: The Afroasiatic Roots of Classical Civilization. The Fabrication of Ancient Greece 1785-1985. Vol. 1* (New Brunswick, NJ: Rutgers University Press, 1987).

Bernstein, Peter. *Against the Gods: The Remarkable Story of Risk* (NY: John Wiley and Sons, 1996).

Bhabha, Homi. *The Location of Culture*. (London: Routledge, 1994).

Birns, Nicholas. "The Trojan Myth: Postmodern Reverberations." *Exemplaria* 5, 1 (March 1993) 45-78.

Blau, Herbert. *Blooded Thought: Occasions of Theatre*. (NY: PAJ Books, 1982).

———. *Take up the Bodies: Theater at the Vanishing Point*. (Urbana, IL: University of Illinois Press, 1982).

———. *To All Appearances: Ideology and Performance*. (NY: Routledge, 1992).

Bloom, Harold. *Figures of Capable Imagination*. (NY: Seabury Press, 1976).

———. *Wallace Stevens: The Poems of Our Climate*. (Ithaca: Cornell University Press, 1977).

Blumenberg, Hans. *The Legitimacy of the Modern Age*. trans. Robert M. Wallace (Cambridge, MA: The MIT Press, 1986).

———. *Work on Myth*. trans. Robert M. Wallace. (Cambridge, MA: The MIT Press, 1985).

Bossy, John. *Christianity in the West 1400-1700*. (NY: Oxford University Press, 1989).

———. *The English Catholic Community 1570-1850*. (London: Darton, Longman & Todd, 1976).

Bourdieu, Pierre. *Outline of a Theory of Practice*. trans. Richard Nice (London: Cambridge University Press, 1977).

Bowers, Fredson. "*The Faerie Queene*, Book II: Mordant, Ruddymane, and the Nymph's Well." *English Studies in Honor of James Southal Wilson*. ed. Fredson Bowers (Charlottesville, VA: William Byrd Press, 1951) 243-51.

Boyarin, Daniel. "The Subversion of the Jews: Moses's Veil and the Hermeneutics of Supersession." *Diacritics* 23, 2 (1993) 16-35.

Braden, Gordon. *Renaissance Tragedy and the Senecan Tradition: Anger's Privilege* (New Haven: Yale University Press, 1985).

Brady, Ciaran. "Spenser's Irish Crisis: Humanism and Experience in the 1590s." *Past and Present* 3 (1986) 17-49.

Brooks, Douglas. "Orientals Like Us: Inexplicable Islam and the Staging of the Orient in Elizabethan England" (unpublished essay).

Brown, Theo. *The Fate of the Dead: A Study in the Folk-Eschatology in the West Country after the Reformation* (Cambridge, D.S. Brewer, 1979).

Bruns, Gerald L. *Hermeneutics Ancient and Modern* (New Haven: Yale University Press, 1992).

Burke, Peter. *The Renaissance Sense of the Past* (London: Edward Arnold, 1969).

Bushnell, Rebecca. *The Tragedies of Tyrants: Political Thought and Theater in the English Renaissance.* (Ithaca: Cornell University Press, 1990).

Bynum, Caroline Walker. *The Resurrection of the Body in Western Christianity 200-1336.* (NY: Columbia University Press, 1995).

Callaghan, Dympna. "Re-reading Elizabeth Cary's *The Tragedie of Mariam, Faire Queene of Jewry.*" *Women, "Race," and Writing in the Early-Modern Period.* ed. Margo Hendricks and Patricia Parker (NY: Routledge, 1994) 163-77.

Camden, William. *Remains Concerning Britain.* (1605) ed. R. D. Dunn (Toronto: University of Toronto Press, 1984).

Caruth, Cathy. "Unclaimed Experience: Trauma and the Possibility of History." *Yale French Studies* 79 (1991) 181-92.

Cary, Elizabeth. *The Tragedie of Mariam, The Fair Queen of Jewry.* ed. Barry Weller and Margaret W. Ferguson (Berkeley, CA: University of California Press, 1994).

Catherine of Genoa. *Purgation and Purgatory.* trans. Serge Hughes (NY: Paulist Press, 1979).

The Catholic Encyclopedia. ed. Charles G. Herbermann, et al. (NY: Robert Appleton Co., 1907-12).

Cavell, Stanley. *Disowning Knowledge in Six Plays of Shakespeare.* (NY: Cambridge University Press, 1988).

———. *Pursuits of Happiness: The Hollywood Comedy of Remarriage.* (Cambridge, MA: Harvard University Press, 1981).

Chew, Samuel. *The Crescent and the Rose: Islam and England during the Renaissance.* (NY: Oxford University Press, 1937).

Clark, Francis. S.J. *Eucharistic Sacrifice and the Reformation.* (London: Darton, Longman & Todd, 1960).

Clark-Maxwell, (Rev.) Prebendary. "Some Letters of Confraternity" *Archaeologia or, Miscellaneous tracts relating to Antiquity.* 75 (1925) 19-60.

———. "Some Further Letters of Fraternity." *Archaeologia, or, Miscellaneous Tracts relating to Antiquity.* 79 (1929) 179-216.

Clebsch, William A. "The Elizabethans on Luther." *Interpreters of Luther: Essays in Honor of Wilhelm Pauck.* ed. Jaroslav Pelikan (Philadelphia, PA: Fortress Press, 1968) 97-120.

Collinson, Patrick. *The Birthpangs of Protestant England: Religious and Cultural Change in the Sixteenth and Seventeenth Centuries.* (London: Macmillan Press, 1988).

Copjec, Joan. *Read My Desire: Lacan against the Historicists.* (Cambridge, MA: The MIT Press, 1994).

Corns, Thomas N. "'Varnish on a Harlot's Cheek': John Milton and the Hierarchies of Secular and Divine Literature." *Sacred and Profane: Secular and Devotional Interplay in early modern British Literature.* ed. Helen Wilcox, et al. (Amsterdam: VU University Press, 1996) 275-81.

Cosin, John. *A Scholastical History of the Canon of the Holy Scripture or the Certain and Indubitate Books thereof as they are Received in the Church of England.* (London, 1657).

Coughlan, Patricia (ed.) *Spenser and Ireland: An Interdisciplinary Perspective.* (Cork: Cork University Press, 1989).

Craig, Joanne. "The Image of Mortality: Myth and History in *The Faerie Queene*." *ELH: English Literary History* 39 (1972) 520-44.

Crosby, Alfred W. *The Measure of Reality: Quantification and Western Society. 1250-1600*. (NY: Cambridge University Press, 1997).

Daston, Lorraine J. "The Domestication of Risk: Mathematical Probability and Insurance 1650-1830." *The Probalistic Revolution*. ed. Lorenz Kruger, et al. (Cambridge, MA: The MIT Press, 1987) 237-60.

Davies, Horton. *Worship and Theology in England: From Cranmer to Baxter and Fox, 1534-1690*. (Grand Rapids, MI: William B. Eerdmans Publishing Co., 1996).

Deane, Thomas. *The Religion of Martin Luther Neither Catholick nor Protestant, Prov'd from his own Works*. (London, 1688).

de Certeau, Michel. *The Writing of History*. trans. Tom Conley (NY: Columbia University Press, 1988).

Delbanco, Andrew. *The Death of Satan: How Americans Have Lost the Sense of Evil*. (NY: Farrar, Straus and Giroux, 1996).

Delumeau, Jean. *Catholicism between Luther and Voltaire: a new view of the Counter-Reformation*. trans. Jeremy Moiser. (London: Burns & Oates, 1977).

Denton, Robert C. *The Apocrypha, Bridge of the Testaments: A Reader's Guide to the Apocryphal Books of the Old Testament*. (Greenwich, CT: Seabury Press, 1954).

Derrida, Jacques. "The Theater of Cruelty and the Closure of Representation." *Writing and Difference*. trans. Alan Bass (Chicago: University of Chicago Press, 1978) 232-50.

———. "White Mythology: Metaphor in the Text of Philosophy." *Margins of Philosophy*. trans. Alan Bass (Chicago: University of Chicago Press, 1982) 207-71.

A Dictionary of the Bible, Dealing with its Language, Literature, and Contents. ed. James Hastings, et al. (NY: Charles Scribner's Sons, 1900).

Dollimore, Jonathan. "Shakespeare, Cultural Materialism, Feminism and Marxist Humanism." *New Literary History* 21, 3 (1990) 471-93.

———. "Two concepts of mimesis: Renaissance literary theory and *The Revenger's Tragedy*." *Drama and Mimesis: Themes in Drama*. Vol. 2. ed. James Redmond (NY: Cambridge University Press, 1990) 25-50.

Douglas, Mary. *Implicit Meanings: Essays in Anthropology*. (1975) (NY: Routledge, 1991).

———. *Natural Symbols: Explorations in Cosmology*. (1970) (NY: Pantheon, 1982).

———. *Purity and Danger: An Analysis of the Concepts of Pollution and Taboo*. (1966) (London: Routledge and Kegan Paul, 1979).

Doyle, A.I., et al. *Manuscript to Print: Tradition and Innovation in the Renaissance Book*. (Durham: Durham University Library Guides, 1975).

Duffy, Eamon. *The Stripping of the Altars*. (New Haven: Yale University Press, 1992).

———. "William, Cardinal Allen, 1532-1594." *Recusant History* 22,3 (1995) 265-90.

Eisenstein, Elizabeth L. *The printing press as an agent of change. Volumes I and II*. (NY: Cambridge University Press, 1994).

Elias, Norbert. *The Civilizing Process. Vol. 2.* trans. Edmund Jephcott (Oxford: Basil Blackwell, 1982).

The Encyclopedia of the Jewish Religion. (new rev. ed.) ed. R.J. Zwi Werblowsky (NY: Adama Books, 1986).

Engels, Wiliam. *Mapping Mortality: The Persistence of Memory and Melancholy in Early Modern England.* (Amherst: University of Massachusetts Press, 1995).

Evelyn, John. *The History of Sabatai Sevi, The Suppos'd Messiah of the Jews (1669).* Reprint of Evelyn's *History of three late famous Impostors.* The Augustan Reprint Society. No. 131. introduction by Christopher Grose (Los Angeles, CA: William Andrews Clark Memorial Library, 1968).

Falco, Raphael. *Conceived Presences: Literary Genealogy in Renaissance England.* (Amherst: University of Massachusetts Press, 1994).

Fallon, Stephen. "The Metaphysics of Milton's divorce tracts." *Politics, Poetics, and hermeneutics in Milton's prose.* ed. David Loewenstein and James Grantham Turner (NY: Cambridge University Press, 1990) 69-83.

Faulkner, J.A. "Luther and the Lord's Supper in the Critical Years 1517-22." *Lutheran Quarterly* 45 (1915) 202-16.

———. "Luther and the Real Presence." *American Journal of Theology* 21 (1917) 225-39.

Ferguson, Arthur. *Clio Unbound: Perceptions of the social and cultural past in Renaissance England.* (Durham, NC: Duke University Press, 1979).

Ferguson, Margaret W. "Running on With Almost Public Voice: The Case of 'E.C.'" *Tradition and the Talents of Women.* ed. Florence Howe (Urbana, IL: U Illinois Press, 1991) 37-67.

Fergusson, Francis. *The Idea of a Theater* (Princeton: Princeton University Press, 1949).

Finke, Laurie A. "Spenser for Hire: Arthurian History as Cultural Capital in *The Faerie Queene.*" *Culture and the King: The Social Implications of the Arthurian Legend.* ed. Martin B. Shichtman and James P. Carley (Albany, NY: SUNY Press, 1994) 211-33.

Fischer, Sandra K. "Elizabeth Cary and Tyranny, Domestic and Religious." *Silent But for the Word: Tudor Women as Patrons, Translators and Writers of Religious Works.* ed. Margaret P. Hannay (Kent, OH: Kent State University Press, 1985). 225-37.

Fish, Stanley. "Wanting a Supplement: the question of interpretation in Milton's early prose." *Politics, poetics, and hermeneutics in Milton's prose.* ed. David Loewenstein and James Grantham Turner. (NY: Cambridge University Press, 1990) 41-68.

Fleissner, Robert F. "*Hamlet* and *The Supplication of Souls* Reconvened." *Notes and Queries* (March 1985) 49-51.

Fletcher, H.F. *Milton's Rabbinical Readings.* (Urbana, IL: University of Illinois Press, 1930).

———. *Milton's Semitic Studies, and Some Manifestations of them in His Poetry.* (Chicago, IL: University of Chicago Press, 1926).

Floyd, John. *Purgatories Triumph over Hell (1613). English Recusant Literature 1558-1640. Vol. 142.* ed. D.M. Rogers (London: The Scolar Press, 1973).

Foster, Donald W. "Resurrecting the Author: Elizabeth Tanfield Cary." *Privileging Gender in Early-Modern England.* ed. Jean Brink. *Sixteenth Century Essays and Studies. Vol. 23* (Kirksville, MO: Northeast Missouri State University Press, 1993) 141-73.

Foucault, Michel. *The Order of Things: An Archaeology of the Human Sciences.* (NY: Random House, 1970).

Foxe, John. *The Acts and Monuments of John Foxe.* ed. George Townsend (NY: AMS Press, 1965).

Fowler, Alastair. "The Image of Mortality: *The Faerie Queene,* II.i-ii." Rpt. in *Essential Articles for the Study of Edmund Spenser.* ed. A.C. Hamilton (Hamden, CT: Archon Books, 1972) 139-52.

————. *Time's Purpled Masquers: Stars and the Afterlife in Renaissance English Literature* (Oxford: Clarendon University Press, 1996).

Freud, Sigmund. *Civilization and its Discontents.* trans. Joan Riviere (London: Hogarth Press, 1939).

————. *Moses and Monotheism.* trans. Katherine Jones (NY: Vintage Books, 1967).

Friedman, Jerome. *The Most Ancient Testimony: Sixteenth-Century Christian-Hebraica in the Age of Renaissance Nostalgia* (Athens: Ohio University Press, 1983).

Frye, Northrop. *Anatomy of Criticism: Four Essays.* (Princeton: Princeton University Press, 1957).

————. *Fables of Identity: Studies in Poetic Mythology.* (NY: Harcourt Brace Jovanovich, 1963).

————. *The Secular Scripture: A Study of the Structure of Romance.* (Cambridge, MA: Harvard University Press, 1976).

Frye, Roland. "The Prince amid the Tombs." *The Renaissance Hamlet.* (Princeton: Princeton University Press, 1984) 205-53.

Fussner, F. Smith. *The Historical Revolution: English Historical Writing and Thought 1580-1640* (London: Routledge & Kegan Paul, 1962).

Garber, Marjorie. "*Hamlet*: Giving up the Ghost." *Hamlet.* ed. Susanne L. Wofford (Boston: St. Martin's Press, 1994) 297-331.

Gebauer, Gunter and Christoph Wulf. *Mimesis: Culture–Art–Society.* trans. Don Reneau (Berkeley: University of California Press, 1995).

Gellner, Ernest. *Thought and Change.* (London: Weidenfield and Nicholson, 1964).

Gibbons, Brian. *Shakespeare and Multiplicity.* (NY: Cambridge University Press, 1993).

Gilman, Ernest B. *Iconoclasm and Poetry in the English Reformation: Down Went Dagon.* (Chicago: University of Chicago Press, 1986).

Gilroy, Paul. *The Black Atlantic: Modernity and Double-Consciousness.* (Cambridge, MA: Harvard University Press, 1994).

Goering, Joseph. "The Invention of Transubstantiation." *Traditio: Studies in Ancient and Medieval History, Thought, and Religion.* 46 (1991) 147-70.

Greenblatt, Stephen. "Remnants of the Sacred in Early Modern England." *Subject and Object in Renaissance Culture.* ed. Margreta De Grazia, et al. (NY: Cambridge University Press, 1996) 337-45.

————. *Renaissance Self-Fashioning From More to Shakespeare.* (Chicago: University of Chicago Press, 1980).

————. *Shakespearean Negotiations: The Circulation of Social Energy in Renaissance England*. (Berkeley: University of California Press, 1988).

Greene, Thomas M. *The Light in Troy: Imitation and Discovery in Renaissance Poetry*. (New Haven: Yale University Press, 1982).

————. "Post-Feudal Rhetoric and Historical Semiotics." *Poetry and Epistemology: Turning points in the history of poetic knowledge; papers from the International Poetry Symposium*. ed. Roland Hagenbuchle and Laura Skandera (Germany: Verlang, 1996) 46-56.

————. "Ritual and Text in the Renaissance." *Canadian Review of Comparative Literature* 18:2-3 (June-September 1991) 179-97.

Greenslade, S.L. (ed.) *The Cambridge History of the Bible. The West from the Reformation to the Present Day*. (NY and London: Cambridge University Press, 1963)

Greg, W.W. "Hamlet's Hallucination." *Modern Language Review* 12, 4 (1917) 393-421.

Gross, Kenneth. *Spenserian Poetics: Idolatry, Iconoclasm & Magic*. (Ithaca: Cornell University Press, 1985).

Grossman, Marshall. "Servile/ Sterile/Style: Milton and the Question of Woman." *Milton and the Idea of Woman*. ed. Julia M. Walker (Urbana, IL: University of Chicago Press, 1988) 148-68.

Guild, William. *Three Rare Monuments of Antiquitie, or Bertram, Priest, a French-Man, of the Bodie and Blood of Christ (written 800 years agoe) Aelfricus, Arch-Bishop of Canterburie, an English-man (His sermon of the Sacrament (preached 627 years agoe:) and Maurus, Abbot, a Scots-man, His discourse of the same (820 years agoe:) All stronglie convincing that grosse Errour of Transubstantiation*. (Aberdeen, 1624).

Guillory, John. *Poetic Authority: Spenser, Milton, and Literary History*. (NY: Columbia University Press, 1983).

Guttierez, Nancy H. "Valuing *Mariam*." *Tulsa Studies in Women's Literature* 10,2 (1991) 233-51.

Hacking, Ian. *The Emergence of Probability: A Philosophical Study of Early Ideas about Probability, Induction and Statistical Inference*. (London and NY: Cambridge University Press, 1975).

Haigh, Christopher. "The Recent Historiography of the English Reformation." *Reformation to Revolution: Politics and religion in early modern England*. ed. Margaret Todd (NY: Routledge, 1995) 13-32.

Halkett, John. *Milton and the Idea of Matrimony: A Study of the Divorce Tracts and Paradise Lost*. (New Haven: Yale University Press, 1970).

Hall, Basil. "The Early Rise and Gradual Decline of Lutheranism in England (1520-1600)." *Reform and Reformation: England and the Continent c 1500-c 1750*. ed. Derek Baker (Oxford: Basil Blackwell, 1979) 103-31.

Halmos, Paul. *Solitude and Privacy: A Study of Social Isolation, its Causes and Therapy*. (London: Routledge & Kegan Paul, 1952).

Hardison, O.B. Jr. *Christian Rite and Christian Drama in the Middle Ages: Essays in the Origin and Early History of Modern Drama*. (Baltimore: Johns Hopkins University Press, 1965).

Hartman, Geoffrey H. and Sanford Budick (eds.) *Midrash and Literature*. (New Haven: Yale University Press, 1986).

Hawkins, Allan (Rev.). Letter. *The New York Times*. 24 November 1995.

Hay, Cynthia (ed.) *Mathematics from Manuscript to Print*. (NY: Oxford University Press, 1988).

Herberle, Mark. "Pagans and Saracens in Spenser's *The Faerie Queene*." *Comparative Literature East and West: Traditions and Trends*. ed. Cornelia N. Moore and Raymond Moody (Honolulu: University of Hawaii Press, 1989) 81-87.

Helgerson, Richard. *Forms of Nationhood: The Elizabethan Writing of England*. (Chicago: University of Chicago Press, 1992).

———. "Inventing Noplace: Or, the Power of Negative Thinking." *The Power of Forms in the English Renaissance*. ed. Stephen J. Greenblatt (Norman, OK: Pilgrim Books, 1982) 101-21.

Hillman, Richard. "'Not Amurath an Amurath Succeeds': Playing Doubles in Shakespeare's *Henriad*." *English Literary Renaissance* 21, 2 (1991) 161-89.

Hirsch, Rudolf. *Printing, Selling, and Reading 1450-1550*. (Wiesbaden: Otto Harrassowitz, 1967).

Hodgson, Margaret T. *Early Anthropology in the Sixteenth and Seventeenth Centuries*. (Philadelphia: University of Pennsylvania Press, 1971).

Hough, Graham. *A Preface to The Faerie Queene*. (NY: W.W. Norton, 1962).

Idel, Moshe. *Golem: Jewish Magical and Mystical Traditions on the Artificial Anthropoid*. (Albany, NY: SUNY Press, 1990).

Ingebretsen, Edward. *Maps of Heaven, Maps of Hell*. (Armonk, NY: M.E. Sharpe Inc., 1996).

Isaac, Erich. "God's Acre." *Landscape* 13 (Winter 1964-65) 28-32.

———. "Religious Geography and the Geography of Religion." *Man and the Earth. University of Colorado Studies, Series in Earth Science*. No. 3 (Boulder: University of Colorado Press, 1965) 1-14.

The Interpreter's Bible. 12 volumes. George Arthur Buttrick, et al. (NY: Abigdon, 1955).

Johnson, Samuel. *The Absolute Impossibility of Transubstantiation Demonstrated*. (London, 1688).

———. *Purgatory prov'd by miracles collected out of Roman-Catholick Authors*. (London, 1688).

Kamuf, Peggy. "Penelope at Work: Interruptions in *A Room of One's Own*." *Novel: A Forum on Fiction* 16 (1982) 5-18.

Kaye, Jacqueline. "Islamic Imperialism and the Creation of Some Ideas of 'Europe.'" *Europe and its Others. Proceedings of the Essex Conference on the Sociology of Literature*. ed. Francis Barker, et al. (Colchester: University of Essex, 1985) 59-71.

Kelley, Donald R. *Foundations of Modern Historical Scholarship: Language, Law, and History in the French Renaissance*. (NY: Columbia University Press, 1970).

Kermode, Frank. "The Canon." *The Literary Guide to the Bible*. ed. Frank Kermode and Robert Alter (Cambridge, MA: Harvard University Press, 1987) 600-610.

Kernodle, George Riley. *From Art to Theatre: Form and Convention in the Renaissance* (Chicago: University of Chicago Press, 1944).

King, John. *Spenser's Poetry and the Reformation Tradition*. (Princeton: Princeton University Press, 1990).

Knapp, Jeffrey. *An Empire Nowhere: England, America, and Literature from Utopia to The Tempest.* (Berkeley: University of California Press, 1992).

Knapp, Robert S. *Shakespeare: The Theater and the Book.* (Princeton: Princeton University Press, 1989).

Kreager, Philip. "New Light on Graunt." *Population Studies* 42 (1988) 129-40.

Krieder, Alan. *English Chantries: The Road to Dissolution.*(Cambridge: Harvard University Press, 1979).

Kristeva, Julia. "Holbein's Dead Christ." *Fragments for a History of the Human Body. Part One.* ed. Michael Feher (NY: Zone Books, 1990) 238-69.

Lacan, Jacques. "The circuit." *The Seminar of Jacques Lacan. Book II.* ed. Jacques-Alain Miller. trans. Sylvana Tomaselli (NY and London: W.W. Norton, 1991) 77-90.

———. "The mirror stage as formative of the function of the I as revealed in psychoanalytic experience." *Ecrits: A Selection.* trans. Alan Sheridan (NY: W.W. Norton, 1977) 1-7.

Lacoue-Labarthe, Philippe. "Theatricum Analyticum." *Glyph* 2 (1977) 122-43.

Lawrence, W.W. "The Play Scene in *Hamlet.*" *Journal of English and Germanic Philology* 18 (1919) 1-22.

Lechmere, John. *The Relection of a Conference Touching the Reall Presence. (1635) English Recusant Literature 1558-1640.* Vol. 249. D. M. Rogers (ed.) (London: The Scolar Press, 1975).

Le Goff, Jacques. *The Birth of Purgatory.* trans. Arthur Goldhammer (Chicago: University of Chicago Press, 1984).

Levine, Joseph M. *Humanism and History: Origins of Modern English Historiography.* (Ithaca: Cornell University Press, 1987).

Levi-Strauss, Claude. *Structural Anthropology. Vol. 2.* trans. Monique Layton (Chicago: University of Chicago Press, 1983).

Levy, F.J. *Tudor Historical Thought.* (San Marino, CA: The Huntington Library, 1967).

Lewalski, Barbara. *Writing Women in Jacobean England.* (Cambridge, MA: Harvard University Press, 1993).

Lewis, C. S. *The Allegory of Love: A Study in Medieval Tradition.* (1936) (London: Oxford University Press, 1959).

Lewis, William. "Playing with Fire and Brimstone: *Auctor Ludens, Diabolus Ludicrus.*" *Auctor Ludens: Essays on Play in Literature.* ed. Gerald Guinness and Andrew Hurley (Philadelphia, PA: John Benjamins Publishing Co., 1986) 47-61.

Lodge, Thomas. (trans.) *The Famous and Memorable Workes of Josephus.* (London, 1602).

Loewenstein, David. *Milton and the Drama of History: Historical Vision, Iconoclasm and the Literary Imagination.* (NY: Cambridge, 1990).

Lupton, Julia Reinhard. *Afterlives of the Saints: Hagiography, Typology, and Renaissance Literature.* (Stanford, CA: Stanford University Press, 1996).

Lyons, John D. and Stephen G. Nichols, Jr. (eds.) *Mimesis: From Mirror to Method: Augustine to Descartes.* (Hanover, NH: University Press of New England, 1982).

MacCaffrey, Isabel Gamble. *Paradise Lost as "Myth."* (Cambridge: Harvard University Press, 1959).

Manley, Lawrence. *Convention 1500-1700.* (Cambridge, MA: Harvard University Press, 1980).

Matar, N.I. "Islam in Interregnum and Restoration England." *The Seventeenth Century* 6,1 (Spring 1991) 57-71.

Matheson, Mark. "*Hamlet* and 'A Matter Tender and Dangerous.'" *Shakespeare Quarterly* 46, 4 (1995) 383-97.

May, Robert. "The Idea of History in Psychoanalysis: Freud and the 'Wolf-man.'" *Psychoanalytic Psychology* 7, 2 (1990) 163-83.

Mazzaro, Jerome. *Transformations in the Renaissance English Lyric.* (Ithaca: Cornell University Press, 1970).

Mazzola, Elizabeth. "Marrying Medusa: Spenser's *Epithalamion* and Renaissance Reconstructions of Female Privacy." *Genre* 25 (1992) 193-210.

―――. "Spenser and Slavery: Faeryland as Black Hole." (unpublished essay).

McCabe, Richard. *The Pillars of Eternity: Time and Providence in The Faerie Queene.* (Dublin: Irish Academic Press, 1989).

McGrath, Alister. *Reformation Thought: An Introduction.* (second ed.) (Cambridge, MA: Blackwell, 1993).

Mehl, Dieter. *The Elizabethan Dumb Show: The History of a Dramatic Convention.* (Cambridge, MA: Harvard University Press, 1966).

Meyer, Kuno (ed.) *Imram Brain, The Voyage of Bran, son of Febel, to the Land of the Living; an old Irish saga, now first edited, with translation, notes, and glossary (1895-97).* (NY: AMS Press, 1972).

Mignolo, Walter. *The Darker Side of the Renaissance: Literacy, Territoriality, & Colonization.* (Ann Arbor, MI: University of Michigan Press, 1995).

Miller, David Lee. *The Poem's Two Bodies: The Poetics of the 1590 Faerie Queene.* (Princeton: Princeton University Press, 1988).

Miller, Lewis H. Jr. "A Secular Reading of *The Faerie Queene*, Book II." *Critical Essays on Spenser from ELH.* (Baltimore: Johns Hopkins University Press, 1970) 206-21.

Milton, John. *The Complete Prose Works of John Milton. Volume Two. 1643-1648.* ed. Ernest Sirluck (New Haven: Yale University Press, 1959).

―――. *Complete Poems and Major Prose.* ed. Merritt Hughes (NY: Macmillan, 1985).

Mollenkott, Virginia R. "The Pervasive Influence of the Apocrypha in Milton's Thought and Art." *Milton and the Art of Sacred Song.* ed. J. Max Patrick and Roger H. Sundell (Madison: University of Wisconsin Press, 1979). 23-43.

Montrose, Louis Adrian. "The Purpose of Playing: Reflections on A Shakespearean Anthropology." *Helios* 7,2 (Spring 1980) 51-74.

Mullaney, Steven. "Strange Things, Gross Terms, Curious Customs: The Rehearsal of Cultures in the Late Renaissance." *Representing the English Renaissance.* ed. Stephen J. Greenblatt (Berkeley: University of California Press, 1988) 65-92.

Nairn, Tom. *The Break-up of Britain.* (London: New Left Books, 1977).

Neibuhr, Gustav. "Lutherans Considering Sweeping Change." *The New York Times*. 18 August 1997. A:10.

Nestrick, William V. "Notable Prosopopeias: Phaedria and Cymochles." *Spenser at Kalamazoo 1983*. ed. Francis Greco (Clarion, Pennsylvania: Clarion University of Pennsylvania, 1983) 57-71.

The New Catholic Encyclopedia. 17 volumes. Prepared by an editorial staff at the Catholic University of America (Palatine, IL: J. Heraty, 1981).

Nohrnberg, James. *The Analogy of The Faerie Queene*. (Princeton: Princeton University Press, 1976).

Nyquist, Mary. "The genesis of gendered subjectivity in the divorce tracts and in *Paradise Lost*." *Remembering Milton: Essays on the Texts and Traditions*. ed. Mary Nyquist and Margaret W. Ferguson (NY: Methuen, 1988) 99-127.

Oakeshott, Michael. *Experience and its Modes* (London: Cambridge University Press, 1933).

Oberman, Heiko A. *The Roots of Anti-Semitism in the Age of Renaissance and Reformation*. (1981) trans. James I. Porter (Philadelphia: Fortress Press, 1984).

Owen, Eivion. "Milton and Selden on Divorce." *Studies in Philology* 43 (1946) 233-57.

The Oxford Dictionary of the Jewish Religion. ed. R.J. Zwi Werblowsky, et al. (NY: Oxford, 1997).

Ozment, Steven. *The Age of Reform 1250-1550: An Intellectual and Religious History of Late Medieval and Reformation Europe*. (New Haven: Yale University Press, 1980).

Panofsky, Ernst. "Comments on Art and Reformation." *Symbols in Transformation: Iconographic Themes at the Time of the Reformation*. ed. Craig Harbison (Princeton: Princeton University Press, 1969) 9-15.

Parker, Patricia. *Inescapable Romance: Studies in the Poetics of a Mode*. (Princeton: Princeton University Press, 1979).

———. "Romance and Empire: Anachronistic *Cymbeline*." *Unfolded Tales: Essays on Renaissance Romance*. ed. George M. Logan and Gordon Teskey (Ithaca: Cornell University Press, 1989) 189-207.

The Passing of Arthur: New Essays in Arthurian Tradition. ed. Christopher Baswell and William Sharpe (NY: Garland, 1988).

Patch, Howard Rollins. *The Other World, According to Descriptions in Medieval Literature*. (Cambridge: Harvard University Press, 1950).

Patrides, C.A. "'The Bloody and Cruell Turke': The Background of a Renaissance Commonplace." *Studies in the Renaissance* 10 (1963) 126-35.

Patterson, Annabel. "No Mere Amatorious Novel?" *Politics, poetics, and hermeneutics in Milton's prose*. ed. David Loewenstein and James Grantham Turner (NY: Cambridge University Press, 1990) 85-101.

Pearse, Nancy Cotton. "Elizabeth Cary: Renaissance Playwright." *Texas Studies in Literature and Language* 18 (1977) 601-08.

Pelikan, Jaroslav. *Reformation of Church and Dogma 1300-1700. The Christian Tradition: A History of the Development of Doctrine*. (Chicago: University of Chicago Press, 1985).

Phillips, John. *The Reformation of Images: Destruction of Art in England 1535-1660*. (Berkeley: University of California Press, 1973).

Pigman, G.W. III. "Imitation and the Renaissance Sense of the Past: the reception of Erasmus' *Ciceronianus*." *Journal of Medieval and Renaissance Studies* 9, 2 (Fall 1979) 155-77.

Powicke, Maurice. *The Reformation in England*. (London: Oxford University Press, 1961).

Quint, David. "'Alexander the Pig': Shakespeare on History and Poetry." *Boundary 2* 10,3 (Spring 1982) 49-67.

———. "Epic and Empire." *Comparative Literature* 41, 1 (Winter 1989) 1-32.

———. *Epic and Empire: Politics and Generic Form from Virgil to Milton*. (Princeton: Princeton University Press, 1993).

Rackin, Phyllis. "Anti-Historians: Women's Roles in Shakespeare's Histories." *Theater Journal* 37, 3 (1985) 329-44.

Reiss, Timothy. *The Discourse of Modernism*. (Ithaca: Cornell University Press, 1982).

———. *Knowledge, Discovery and Imagination in Early Modern Europe*. (NY: Cambridge University Press, 1997).

———. *Tragedy and Truth: Studies in the Development of a Renaissance and Neoclassical Discourse*. (New Haven: Yale University Press, 1980).

Renan, Ernest. "What is a Nation?" trans. Martin Thom. *Nation and Narration*. ed. Homi Bhabha (London and NY: Routledge, 1990) 8-22.

Rosenblatt, Jason. *Torah and Law in Paradise Lost*. (Princeton: Princeton University Press, 1994).

Ross, Malcolm Mackenzie. *Poetry and Dogma: The Transfiguration of Eucharistic Symbols in Seventeenth Century English Poetry*. (New Brunswick, NJ: Rutgers University Press, 1954).

Rotman, Brian. *Signifying Nothing: The Semiotics of Zero*. (NY: St Martin's Press, 1987).

Rutledge, Douglas F., ed. *Ceremony and Text in the Renaissance*. (Newark: University of Delaware Press, 1996).

Said, Edward. *Orientalism*. (NY: Random House, 1978).

Sasse, Herman. *This is my body: Luther's contention for the Real Presence in the Sacrament of the Altar*. (Minneapolis: Augsburg Publishing House, 1959).

Saurat, Denis. *Milton: Man and Thinker*. (NY: Haskell House, 1970).

Schillebeeckx, Edward, O.P. and Boniface Willems, O.P. (eds.) *The Problem of Eschatology. Concilium: Theology in the Age of Renewal. Vol. 41.* (NY: Paulist Press, 1969).

Scholem, Gershom. *The Messianic Idea in Judaism, and Other Essays on Jewish Spirituality*. (NY: Schocken Books, 1971).

———. *Sabbatai Sevi: The Mystical Messiah 1626-1676*. (Princeton: Princeton University Press, 1973).

Schwartz, Regina. *Remembering & Repeating in Milton's Theology and Poetics* (Chicago: University of Chicago Press, 1993).

Schwoebel, Robert. *The Shadow of the Crescent: The Renaissance Image of the Turk (1453-1517)*. (Nieuwkoop: B. DeGraaf, 1967).

Setton, Kenneth M. "Lutheranism and the Turkish Peril." *Balkan Studies* (1962) 133-68.

Shakespeare, William. *Antony and Cleopatra*. ed. M.R. Ridley (London: Routledge, 1991).

————. *Coriolanus*. ed. Philip Brockbank (London: Routledge, 1990).

————. *Hamlet*. ed. Harold Jenkins (London: Routledge, 1993).

————. *King Henry IV Part 1*. ed. A.R. Humphreys (NY: Routledge, 1989).

————. *Othello*. ed. M.R. Ridley (London and New York: Routledge, 1993).

————. *Sonnets*. ed. Stephen Booth (New Haven: Yale University Press, 1977).

Shershow, Scott Cutler. "'The Mouth of hem All': Ben Jonson, Authorship, and the Performing Object." *Theatre Journal* 46, 2 (1994) 187-212.

Shuger, Deborah K. *Habits of Thought in the English Renaissance: Religion, Politics, & the Dominant Culture*. (Berkeley: University of California Press, 1990).

————. "'Nor th' exterior nor the inward man resembles what it was': *Hamlet* and Christianity." (unpublished essay).

————. *The Renaissance Bible: Scholarship, Sacrifice, and Subjectivity*. (Berkeley: University of California Press, 1994).

Sidney, Philip. *A Defence of Poetry*. ed. J.A. Van Dorsten (NY: Oxford University Press, 1986).

Silberman, Lauren. "*The Faerie Queene*, Book II and the Limitations of Temperance." *Modern Language Studies* 17 (Fall 1987) 9-22.

Slavin, Arthur J. "The Gutenberg Galaxy and the Tudor Revolution." *Print and Culture in the Renaissance. Essays on the Advent of Printing in Europe*. ed. Gerald P. Tyson and Sylvia S. Wagonheim (Newark: University of Delaware Press, 1986) 90-109.

Smith, Jonathan Z. *Imagining Religion: From Babylon to Jonestown*. (Chicago: University of Chicago Press, 1980).

Smith, Preserved. *A Short History of Christian Theophagy*. (Chicago: The Open Court Publishing Co., 1922).

Somerville, C. John. *The Secularization of Early Modern England: From Religious Culture to Religious Faith*. (NY: Oxford University Press, 1992).

Sopher, David E. *Geography of Religions*. (Englewood Cliffs, NJ: Prentice-Hall, 1967).

Southern, R.W. *Western Views of Islam in the Middle Ages*. (Cambridge: Harvard University Press, 1962).

Spencer, Terence. "Turks and Trojans in the Renaissance." *Modern Language Review* 47 (1952) 330-33.

Spenser, Edmund. *A View of the Present State of Ireland*. ed. W. L. Renwick (London: Eric Partridge, 1934).

————. *The Yale Edition of the Shorter Poems of Edmund Spenser*. ed. William A. Oram, et al. (New Haven: Yale University Press, 1989).

————. *The Faerie Queene*. A.C. Hamilton (ed.) (NY: Longman, 1987).

————. *The Works of Edmund Spenser: A Variorum Edition*. 11 volumes. ed. Edwin Greenlaw, et al. (Baltimore: Johns Hopkins University Press, 1932-57).

Sperber, Dan. *Rethinking Symbolism*. trans. Alice L. Morton (London: Cambridge University Press, 1975).

Stallybrass, Peter. "Patriarchal Territories: The Body Enclosed." *Rewriting the Renaissance: The Discourses of Sexual Difference in Early Modern Europe*. ed.

Margaret W. Ferguson, Maureen Quilligan, and Nancy Vickers (Chicago: University of Chicago Press, 1986) 123-42.

Stern, Menahem. "Josephus and the Roman Empire as Reflected in *The Jewish War.*" *Josephus, Judaism, and Christianity.* ed. Louis H. Feldman (Detroit, MI: Wayne State University Press, 1987) 71-80.

Stevens, Wallace. *The Palm at the End of the Mind: Selected Poems and a Play.* ed. Holly Stevens (Hamden, CT: Archon Books, 1984).

Stollman, Samuel S. "Milton's Rabbinical Readings and Fletcher." *Milton Studies* 4 (1972) 195-213.

Stone, Lawrence. *The Crisis of the Aristocracy 1558-1641* (abr. ed.). (London: Oxford University Press, 1977).

St. Patrick's Purgatory, A Twelfth-Century Tale of a Journey to the Other World (Tractatus de Purgatorio sancti Patricii). trans. Jean-Michel Picard (Ireland: Four Courts Press, 1988).

Straznicky, Marta. "'Profane Stoical Paradoxes': *The Tragedy of Mariam* and Sidnean Closet Drama." *English Literary Renaissance* (1994) 104-34.

Strong, Roy. *The Cult of Elizabeth: Elizabethan Portraiture and Pageantry.* (Berkeley, CA: University of California Press, 1977).

Teskey, Gordon. "Irony, Allegory, and Metaphysical Decay." *PMLA* 109, 3 (Spring 1994) 397-408.

———. "Mutability, Genealogy, and the Authority of Forms." *Representations* 41 (Winter 1993) 104-22

Thomas, D. Keith. *Religion and the Decline of Magic: Studies in Popular Beliefs in Sixteenth- and Seventeenth-Century England.* (NY: Charles Scribner's Sons, 1971).

Thrall, W.F. "Virgil's *Aeneid* and the Irish *Imrama.*" *Modern Philology* 15, 8 (1917) 65-90.

Torrey, Charles Cutler. *Apocryphal Literature: A Brief Introduction.* (New Haven: Yale University Press, 1946).

Travitsky, Betty. "The *Feme Covert* in Elizabeth Cary's *Mariam.*" *Ambiguous Realities: Women in the Middle Ages and Renaissance.* ed. Carole Levin and Jeanie Watson (Detroit, MI: Wayne State University Press, 1987) 184-96.

Tribble, Evelyn B. "The Partial Sign: Spenser and the Sixteenth-Century Crisis of Semiotics." *Ceremony and Text in the Renaissance.* ed. Douglas F. Rutledge (Newark: University of Delaware Press, 1996) 23-34.

Turner, James Grantham. "The Intelligible Flame." *John Milton.* ed. Annabel Patterson (NY: Longman, 1992) 74-86.

———. *One Flesh: Paradisal Marriage and Sexual Relations in the Age of Milton.* (Oxford: Clarendon Press, 1993).

Valbuena, Olga Lucia. "Milton's Divorsive Interpretation and the Gendered Reader." *Milton Studies* 27 (1992) 115-37.

Valency, Maurice J. *The Tragedies of Herod and Mariamne.* (NY: Columbia University Press, 1940).

Van Gennep, Arnold. *The Rites of Passage.* (1908). trans. Monika B. Vizedom and Gabrielle L. Caffee (Chicago: University of Chicago Press, 1960).

Waddington, Raymond. "Lutheran *Hamlet.*" *English Language Notes* 27, 2 (1989) 27-42.

Walker, D.P. *The Decline of Hell: Seventeenth-Century Discussions of Eternal Torment.* (London: Routledge & Kegan Paul, 1964).

Wall, John N., Jr. "The Reformation in England and the Typographical Revolution: 'By this printing . . . the doctrine of the Gospel soundeth to all nations.'" *Print and Culture in the Renaissance: Essays on the Advent of Printing in Europe.* ed. Gerald P. Tyson and Sylvia S. Wagonheim (Newark: University of Delaware Press, 1986) 208-21.

Walton, Brian. *Biblio Sacra Polyglotta.* (London, 1657).

Watson, Robert N. *The Rest is Silence: Death as Annihilation in the English Renaissance.* (Berkeley: University of California Press, 1994).

Way, Albert. "Notice of a Formula of a Papal Indulgence, Printed by Pynson, and of some other documents of like character." *Archaeological Journal* 17 (1860) 25-56.

Weimann, Robert. *Shakespeare and the Popular Tradition in the Theater: Studies in the Social Dimension of Dramatic Form and Function.* (Baltimore: Johns Hopkins University Press, 1978).

Whitaker, Virgil. "The Theological Structure of *The Faerie Queene*, Book 1." *ELH: English Literary History.* 19 (1952) 151-64.

Whitaker, William. *A Disputation on Holy Scripture, against the Papists, especially Bellarmine and Stapleton.* (1588). trans. and ed. for the Parker Society. Vol. 45 (London: Cambridge University Press, 1849).

Whitman, Jon. *Allegory: The Dynamics of an Ancient and Medieval Technique.* (Cambridge, MA: Harvard University Press, 1987).

Wilson, John Dover. *What Happens in "Hamlet."* (NY: Macmillan, 1935).

Wittreich, Joseph. "'Inspir'd with Contradiction': Mapping Gender Discourses in *Paradise Lost.*" *Literary Milton: text, pretext, context.* ed. Diana Trevino Benet and Michael Lieb (Pittsburgh, PA: Duquesne University Press, 1994) 133-60.

Wofford, Susanne. *The Choice of Achilles: The Ideology of Figure in the Epic.* (Stanford, CA: Stanford University Press, 1992).

Wollaeger, Mark. "Apocryphal Narration: Milton, Raphael, and the Book of Tobit." *Milton Studies* 21 (1985) 137-56.

Woodhouse, A.S.P. "Nature and Grace in *The Faerie Queene.*" *ELH: English Literary History* 16, 3 (1949) 194-228.

Wooten, John. "From Purgatory to the Paradise of Fools: Dante, Ariosto and Milton." *ELH: English Literary History* 49 (1982) 741-50.

Wright, Charles and C. Ernest Fayle. *A History of Lloyd's: From the Founding of Lloyd's Coffee House to the Present Day.* (London: Macmillan & Co., 1928).

Yates, Frances. *The Occult Philosophy in the Elizabethan Age.* (London: ARK Paperbacks, 1983).

Yerushalmi, Yosef Hayim. *Freud's Moses: Judaism Terminable and Interminable.* (New Haven: Yale University Press, 1991).

Young, James E. *The Texture of Memory: Holocaust Memorials and Meaning.* (New Haven: Yale University Press, 1993).

Young, Robert. *White Mythologies: Writing History and the West.* (NY: Routledge, 1990).

INDEX OF NAMES AND PLACES

INDEX OF SUBJECTS

Studies in the History of Christian Thought

EDITED BY HEIKO A. OBERMAN

Recent volumes in the series:

Prospectus available on request

BRILL — P.O.B. 9000 — 2300 PA LEIDEN — THE NETHERLANDS